128653

D1137911

REVISE BTEC

Applied Science
Principles of Applied Science
UNIT 1

REVISION WORKBOOK

Series Consultant: Harry Smith   Author: Jennifer Stafford-Brown

- -

THE REVISE BTEC SERIES

Principles of Applied Science Revision Workbook	9781446902783
Principles of Applied Science Revision Guide	9781446902776
Application of Science Revision Workbook	9781446902844
Application of Science Revision Guide	9781446902837

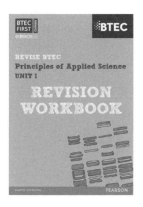   

This Revision Workbook is designed to complement your classroom and home learning, and to help prepare you for the external test. It does not include all the content and skills needed for the complete course. It is designed to work in combination with Edexcel's main BTEC Applied Science 2012 Series.

To find out more visit:
www.pearsonschools.co.uk/BTECsciencerevision

ALWAYS LEARNING   PEARSON

Contents

1-to-1 page match with the Revision Guide ISBN 9781446902776

A small bit of small print

Edexcel publishes Sample Assessment Material and the Specification on its website. This is the official content and this book should be used in conjunction with it. The questions in this book have been written to help you practise every topic in the book. Remember: the real exam questions may not look like this.

Cell structure and function 1

1 Which **one** of the following cells does not have a nucleus?

Put a cross in the box next to the correct answer.   **(1 mark)**

☐ **A** sensory neurone

☐ **B** red blood cell

☐ **C** white blood cell

☐ **D** motor neurone

2 The diagram below shows a sensory neurone cell.

> Choose from these cell parts for the answer:
> * cytoplasm
> * cell membrane
> * nucleus

Identify the parts labelled A to C in the diagram.   **(3 marks)**

A ....

B ....

C ....

Guided

3 Describe how the structures of a plant and animal cell are different.   **(3 marks)**

A plant cell has three different parts compared to an animal cell. These parts are a cell wall

which ....,

chloroplasts which ....,

and vacuoles that... .

> There are 3 marks available for this question so you will need to include 3 different cell parts in your answer to get each of these marks. Also, notice that the key verb is describe which means you have to identify the cell part and also describe the part's function.

Cell structure and function 2

1 Which cell is able to change its shape to get to infected tissues?

Put a cross in the box next to the correct answer. **(1 mark)**

☐ **A** white blood cell

☐ **B** guard cell

☐ **C** root hair cell

☐ **D** sperm cell

2 Describe the function of the following parts of cells:

> Guided

(a) nucleus **(1 mark)**

The nucleus contains genetic information that ....

....

> Guided

(b) cell membrane **(1 mark)**

The cell membrane allows ....

....

(c) mitochondria **(1 mark)**

....

....

> Guided

3 The diagram below shows a root hair cell from a plant.

Explain how the cell's structure helps it to carry out its function. **(4 marks)**

The function of the root hair cell is to absorb .... and ....

The root hair cell has a long extension to give it a ....

....

Plant cell organelles

1   Photosynthesis is the process where plants make their own food using sunlight.
Identify where this process takes place.   **(2 marks)**

....

....

....

2   Describe the functions of a vacuole in a plant cell.   **(2 marks)**

....

....

....

3   The diagram below shows a plant cell.

(a) Identify the name of the plant cell.   **(1 mark)**

....

(b) Describe the function of this plant cell.   **(2 marks)**

....

....

....

Animal cell organelles

1 The diagram below shows a cell from an egg.

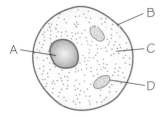

Figure 1

Choose from these cell parts for the answer:
- cytoplasm
- mitochondrion
- nucleus
- cell membrane

Name the parts labelled A–D in the diagram.   **(4 marks)**

A ....

B ....

C ....

D ....

2 Identify three similarities between plant and animal cells.   **(3 marks)**

Plant cells and animal cells both have

1 ....

2 ....

3 ....

3 Describe the function of these parts of animal cells:

> Guided

(a) nucleus   **(1 mark)**

The nucleus contains genetic information that ....

> Guided

(b) cell membrane   **(1 mark)**

The cell membrane controls entry...

(c) cytoplasm   **(1 mark)**

....

Cells, tissues and organs

1 Complete the sentence by putting a cross in the box next to the correct answer.

Cells with similar structures and functions are joined together to make: **(1 mark)**

☐ **A** tissues

☐ **B** cells

☐ **C** plants

☐ **D** mitochondria

> **Guided**

2 Describe what an organ system is. **(2 marks)**

An organ system is a group of .... that work together to

carry out a ....

3 There are many different organ systems in the body.

Describe one organ system. **(2 marks)**

....

....

....

There are lots of different organ systems in the body but you do not need to learn the details of each organ system. Examples of organ systems include:

- immune system
- cardiovascular system
- respiratory system
- nervous system
- endocrine system

- digestive system
- reproductive system
- excretory system
- musculoskeletal system

Function of plant organs

1 Which of the following is an example of a plant organ?

Put a cross in the box next to the correct answer. **(1 mark)**

☐ **A** nucleus   ☐ **B** guard cell

☐ **C** root   ☐ **D** vacuole

> Some of these are examples of plant **cells** or **cell parts,** not organs.

2 Which plant organ carries glucose through a plant?

Put a cross in the box next to the correct answer. **(1 mark)**

☐ **A** xylem   ☐ **B** phloem

☐ **C** root   ☐ **D** leaf

> Remember, xylem carries water and minerals through the plant and roots take in water from the soil.

▷ **Guided** ▷ 3 Describe the function of a leaf. **(3 marks)**

A leaf contains .... which is where ....

.... Leaves are used in plants to produce ....

4 The diagram below shows water travelling from the roots of the plant to the leaves.

(a) Name this process. **(1 mark)**

....

(b) Describe this process. **(3 marks)**

....

....

....

DNA

1   The shape of DNA is sometimes called which **one** of the following?

Put a cross in the box next to the correct answer.   **(1 mark)**

☐   **A**   double helix

☐   **B**   double pump

☐   **C**   single helix

☐   **D**   double arc

Guided   2   **(a)**   State the four base pairs that make up DNA.   **(4 marks)**

1   Adenine

2   ....

3   Guanine

4   ....

(b)   Identify the base pairing of these bases: **(2 marks)**

Adenine pairs with ....

Guanine pairs with ....

> Remember that curly C goes with curly G and straight A with straight T.

3   The diagram below shows a motor neurone.

Cell body   Fatty sheath

Nucleus   Long fibre

Muscle fibres

Dendrites

Label on the diagram where DNA would be found in this cell.   **(1 mark)**

7

Chromosomes and genes

1 How many pairs of chromosomes are in a human cell?

Put a cross in the box next to the correct answer. **(1 mark)**

☐ **A** 13   ☐ **B** 46

☐ **C** 23   ☐ **D** 20

2 Complete the sentence by putting a cross in the box next to the correct answer.

Chromosomes are found in the nucleus of an organism's cells. Chromosomes are made up of: **(1 mark)**

☐ **A** genotype   ☐ **B** phenotype

☐ **C** sugars   ☐ **D** DNA

Guided **3** Describe the function of genes. **(2 marks)**

Genes are short lengths of DNA which give ....

....

4 (a) Identify the male and female gametes. **(2 marks)**

....

....

> Gametes are also called 'sex cells'.

(b) How many chromosomes does each gamete contain? **(1 mark)**

....

> A gamete only contains the genetic information from one parent. In all other cells there are 46 chromosomes, 23 of which are from one parent and 23 from the other parent.

Guided **5** Describe why chromosomes in all cells apart from the gametes are always in pairs? **(2 marks)**

Chromosomes come in pairs as they are inherited from

....

....

Chromosomes

Alleles, genotypes and phenotypes

The image shows chromosomes with alleles for the same gene.

Alleles for the same gene

1   Complete the sentence by putting a cross in the box next to the correct answer.   **(1 mark)**

Alleles for the same gene are known as:

☐   **A**   heterozygous

☐   **B**   homozygous

☐   **C**   genotype

☐   **D**   chromosome

> Homo means the same, hetero means different.

2   **(a)**   Describe what phenotype means.   **(1 mark)**

....

....

> The genotype is the combination of genes an organism has. The phenotype is the combination of characteristics that an organism displays.

(b)   Give an example of a phenotype.   **(1 mark)**

....

....

> Guided

(c)   Explain why there are similarities in phenotypes within families.   **(2 marks)**

A person's phenotype is determined by their .... Genes from parents are

passed onto their ....

> Guided

3   Explain what it means if a person is heterozygous for a gene.   **(2 marks)**

Heterozygous means ...., so if a person is heterozygous for a gene, it means that

they have ....

Punnett squares and pedigree diagrams

1   The offspring of a male and a female will receive one allele from each parent.

Which allele determines the phenotype of the offspring?

Put a cross in the box next to the correct answer.   **(1 mark)**

☐ **A** recessive   ☐ **B** dominant

☐ **C** gamete   ☐ **D** genotype

⟩ **Guided** ⟩   2   Describe what is meant by a recessive allele.   **(2 marks)**

The characteristic from a recessive allele will only be seen if ....

....

3   Whether an individual has dimples is determined by the alleles they inherit from their parents.

A female parent with the genotype Dd has dimples and a male parent with the genotype dd does not have dimples.

(a)   Complete the Punnett square to show the gametes of the parents and the genotypes of the offspring for this male and female.   **(2 marks)**

Female gametes

		D	d
Male gametes	d		
	d		

The dominant allele is shown with a capital letter and the recessive with a lower-case letter.

(b)   State the probability of the offspring having dimples.   **(1 mark)**

....

(c)   What is the percentage probability of a homozygous dominant mother and homozygous recessive father producing a child with dimples?

Put a cross in the box next to the correct answer.   **(1 mark)**

☐ **A** 0%   ☐ **B** 25%

☐ **C** 75%   ☐ **D** 100%

Predicting genetic outcomes

1   An individual's hair colour is determined by the alleles they inherit from their parents.

A female parent with the genotype bb has blonde hair and a male parent with the genotype Bb has brown hair.

Female gametes

(a)   Complete the Punnett square to show the gametes of the parents and the genotypes of the offspring.   **(1 mark)**

(b)   If these two parents have one child, state the probability that this child would have blonde hair.   **(1 mark)**

Male gametes

....

(c)   Give the genetic term that describes the genotype bb.   **(1 mark)**

....

2   Cystic fibrosis is a genetic disorder caused by recessive alleles.

The diagram opposite shows the inheritance of cystic fibrosis in a family.

☐ Male
○ Female
■ ● Affected individual

(a)   Complete the sentence by putting a cross in the box next to the correct answer.

In generation III, affected individual 3 is: **(2 marks)**

☐   **A**   an unaffected female

☐   **B**   heterozygous for cystic fibrosis

☐   **C**   homozygous dominant for cystic fibrosis

☐   **D**   homozygous recessive for cystic fibrosis

〉 Guided 〉 (b)   Explain why pedigree analysis would be important to the unaffected individuals in generation III.   **(5 marks)**

Use percentages or ratios to help back up your explanation.

Individuals 2 and 3 both have the genotype Cc, as they do not have cystic fibrosis but must both have inherited a .... Pedigree analysis will determine the likelihood that their offspring will either inherit or carry cystic fibrosis.

If both parents are heterozygous (Cc), ...

....

If one parent is homozygous dominant (CC) and the other heterozygous (Cc), ...

....

If one parent is homozygous recessive (cc) and the other heterozygous (Cc), ...

....

....

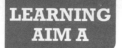

Genetic mutations

> Guided

1 Describe what a mutation is. **(2 marks)**

If part of the base sequence on a DNA molecule ....

....

> Mutations can cause genetic changes in organisms.

2 Identify what can happen to the phenotype of an organism if a genetic mutation occurs. **(1 mark)**

....

3 Sickle cell anaemia is a recessive genetic mutation that has a harmful effect on humans.

   (a) Identify **one** other harmful genetic mutation. **(1 mark)**

   ....

   (b) Describe what is meant by a recessive genetic mutation. **(3 marks)**

   ....

   ....

   ....

Homeostasis

1 Below are four statements about changes in the body.

Put a cross in the box next to the correct statement.   **(1 mark)**

☐ **A** A gene detects changes in the body.

☐ **B** A receptor detects changes in the body.

☐ **C** An effector detects changes in the body.

☐ **D** An affector detects changes in the body.

> If you're not sure, it will help to eliminate the answers which are definitely wrong.

Guided **2** Which **two** systems work together to maintain homeostasis?   **(2 marks)**

1 Nervous system

2 ....

3 The diagram illustrates the feedback mechanism that helps the body to maintain a constant internal environment.

> Think about where the information from the receptor has to go in order to initiate a response.

receptor ⟶ **X** ⟶ effector

Name part X in the diagram.   **(1 mark)**

....

Guided **4** When an individual exercises, their body undergoes a range of changes to cope with the demands of increased activity.

Describe and give reasons for **two** changes which result from exercising.   **(4 marks)**

Exercising causes an increase in the production of carbon dioxide

because ....

....

It also causes body temperature to increase because ....

....

....

....

13

The nervous system

1 The diagrams show two neurones, A and B.

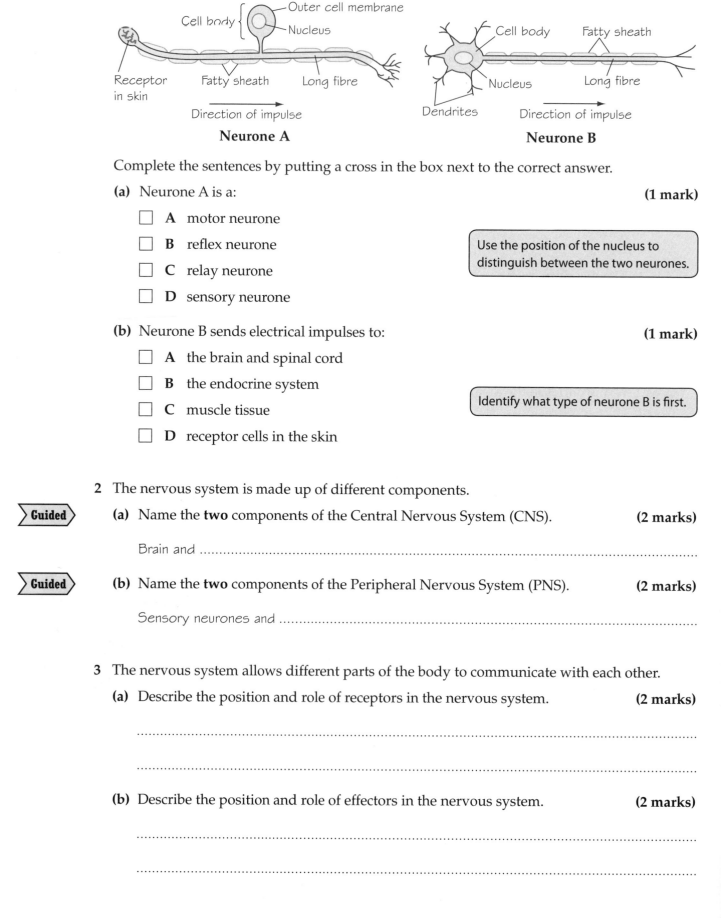

Complete the sentences by putting a cross in the box next to the correct answer.

(a) Neurone A is a: (1 mark)

☐ **A** motor neurone

☐ **B** reflex neurone

☐ **C** relay neurone

☐ **D** sensory neurone

> Use the position of the nucleus to distinguish between the two neurones.

(b) Neurone B sends electrical impulses to: (1 mark)

☐ **A** the brain and spinal cord

☐ **B** the endocrine system

☐ **C** muscle tissue

☐ **D** receptor cells in the skin

> Identify what type of neurone B is first.

2 The nervous system is made up of different components.

> Guided

(a) Name the **two** components of the Central Nervous System (CNS).   (2 marks)

Brain and ....

> Guided

(b) Name the **two** components of the Peripheral Nervous System (PNS).   (2 marks)

Sensory neurones and ....

3 The nervous system allows different parts of the body to communicate with each other.

(a) Describe the position and role of receptors in the nervous system.   (2 marks)

....

....

(b) Describe the position and role of effectors in the nervous system.   (2 marks)

....

....

Involuntary and voluntary responses

1 Complete the sentence by putting a cross in the box next to the correct answer.

   Voluntary response is also called: **(1 mark)**

   ☐ **A** conscious control

   ☐ **B** unconscious control

   ☐ **C** reflex response

   ☐ **D** sensory response

2 Reflex responses are usually there to protect the body from harm.

   (a) Give an example of a reflex response.   **(1 mark)**

   > You will need to be able to explain the difference between reflex and voluntary responses and give examples of each.

   ....

   ....

Guided

   (b) Describe the pathway of a nerve impulse through a reflex arc.   **(3 marks)**

   The receptor cells pick up a .... and transmit an impulse to the

   .... In the CNS the ....

   .... connect via synapses to ....

   The motor neurones then send impulses to the .... to initiate

   a response.

3 Explain the difference in speed between voluntary and involuntary responses.   **(3 marks)**

   ....

   ....

   ....

Synapses

1 Complete the sentence by putting a cross in the box next to the correct answer.

The gap between two neurones is called a: **(1 mark)**

☐ **A** reflex   ☐ **B** synapse

☐ **C** stimulus   ☐ **D** response

> **Guided**

2 The diagram below shows a synapse.

Describe how electrical signals from neurones pass across a synapse.   **(3 marks)**

The electrical impulse reaches the synapse at the end of the neurone. This ....

....

....

3 The diagram opposite shows a sensory neurone.

   (a) Name parts A–D.   **(4 marks)**

   A ....

   B ....

   C ....

   D ....

Direction of impulse

Choose your answer from the following:
- receptor
- cell body
- nucleus
- fatty sheath

> **Guided**

   (b) Explain how information from a receptor is transmitted to the central nervous system.   **(4 marks)**

   The signal travels along the sensory neurones down their ....

   as an electrical .... This travels across ....

   using .... to reach the CNS.

Control of blood glucose

1 Complete the sentence by putting a cross in the box next to the correct answer.

The process of the body keeping the same internal environment is called: **(1 mark)**

☐ **A** thermoregulation   ☐ **B** homeostasis

☐ **C** involuntary response   ☐ **D** homozygous

2 Complete the sentence by putting a cross in the box next to the correct answer.

Excess blood glucose is converted into: **(1 mark)**

☐ **A** glucagon   ☐ **B** glycogen

☐ **C** insulin   ☐ **D** adrenalin

3 A doctor recorded the blood glucose concentration of an individual over an eight-hour period. The results are shown in the table.

Time of day	blood glucose concentration (mg per 100 cm³)
05.00	76
06.00	75
07.00	73
08.00	125
09.00	90
10.00	82
11.00	80
12.00	79
13.00	130

(a) Describe the trend in blood glucose concentration for this eight-hour period.   **(2 marks)**

....

....

> If you are asked to describe a trend you need to say what the trend is and use data to back it up.

....

Guided

(b) Suggest reasons for the changes in blood glucose concentration.   **(3 marks)**

The blood glucose levels go down as the individual has not had ....

.... Then they eat a meal which contains ....

.... so their blood glucose concentration ....

The blood glucose levels then start to ....

Guided

(c) Explain the role of the pancreas in regulating blood glucose.   **(4 marks)**

When blood glucose levels are too high, the pancreas ....

which .... This returns the blood glucose

levels to ....

17

Differences between the endocrine and nervous systems

1 (a) Which target organ responds to the hormone glucagon? **(1 mark)**

....

(b) Describe how a hormone is transmitted to the target organ. **(1 mark)**

....

2 Complete the sentence by putting a cross in the box next to the correct answer. **(1 mark)**

The nervous system transmits impulses by:

☐ **A** electrical and chemical transmission

☐ **B** electrical transmission

☐ **C** chemical and neural transmission

☐ **D** chemical transmission

⟩Guided⟩ 3 The endocrine and nervous systems allow different parts of the body to communicate with each other.

Explain the differences in communication between the endocrine and the nervous systems. **(4 marks)**

The endocrine system transmits signals via a gland secreting a hormone which is carried in

the blood, so the speed of communication is slow. The nervous system ....

....

....

Thermoregulation

1   Which one of the following means an increase in the diameter of blood vessels?

Put a cross in the box next to the correct answer.   **(1 mark)**

☐ **A** vasoconstriction

☐ **B** vasodilation

☐ **C** shivering

☐ **D** sweating

> **Guided**

2   Explain why a person gets goose bumps when they are cold.   **(2 marks)**

Goose bumps make a person's body hair ....

> The question asks you to explain, so state what goose bumps do **and** how this relates to a person feeling cold.

....

....

This helps to reduce heat loss by ....

....

3   Describe how the body detects a change in temperature.   **(4 marks)**

....

....

....

....

4   Explain why it is important for body temperature to stay at 37 °C.   **(2 marks)**

....

....

> **Guided**

5   Describe **two** ways in which the body can try to lose excess body heat.   **(4 marks)**

Sweating helps the body to lose heat by...

....

....

....

Learning aim B: 6-mark questions 1

1 Taking part in sport and exercise is good for a person's health. However, the process of taking part in sports increases the amount of heat a person generates. It is important that the core body temperature remains at 37 °C.

Explain how the body is able to maintain the same internal temperature when taking part in sports activities.   **(6 marks)**

> You will be more successful in extended writing questions if you plan your answer before you start writing. When answering this question, you will need to think about the following:
>
> - How does the body detect the change in temperature and where are these receptors located?
> - What does the body do in order to try to decrease the temperature?
> - What happens when the person stops exercising?
>
> The best answers use accurate technical language where possible. For instance, instead of saying that blood vessels 'widen', you should say that they 'dilate'.

....

....

....

....

....

....

....

....

....

....

....

....

....

....

Learning aim B: 6-mark questions 2

1   The body uses two main methods to communicate with other parts of the body – the nervous system and the endocrine system.

Explain the similarities and differences between these two systems.   **(6 marks)**

> You will be more successful in extended writing questions if you plan your answer before you start writing. When answering this question, you will need to think about the following:
>
> - What is the main purpose of each system?
> - What are the similarities between the two systems?
> - What are the differences between the two systems?
> - When comparing the two systems, have you referred to each system in every point you have made?
>
> The best answers give examples wherever possible. This shows that you have understood the concept that you are explaining.

....

....

....

....

....

....

....

....

....

....

....

....

....

....

....

....

The structure of an atom 1

1   Below are four statements about the mass of a proton.

Put a cross in the box next to the correct statement.   **(1 mark)**

☐   **A**   A proton has no mass

☐   **B**   A proton has a much smaller mass than an electron

☐   **C**   A proton has the same mass as an electron

☐   **D**   A proton has a much larger mass than an electron

> An electron is the smallest particle in an atom.

2   An atom is made up of three different types of particle.

(a)   Name the three particles that make up an atom.   **(3 marks)**

1   ....

2   ....

3   ....

(b)   Which particles are found in the nucleus of an atom?   **(2 marks)**

> There are 2 marks available for this question so there must be 2 particles in the nucleus of an atom.

....

....

3   In the space below, draw a diagram of an atom, including and labelling the following: **(3 marks)**

A   a proton

B   a neutron

C   an electron

The structure of an atom 2

1 (a) What is the charge on an electron? **(1 mark)**

....

(b) What is the charge on a neutron? **(1 mark)**

....

> **Guided**

(c) Describe how electrons are arranged in an atom. **(2 marks)**

Electrons are arranged in ....

....

2 Complete the table below with the missing numbers. **(2 marks)**

Atom	Electrons	Neutrons	Protons
Sodium	11	12	
Oxygen		8	8

3 What is an element made up of? **(1 mark)**

....

4 Identify the number of protons in an atom which has 18 electrons.

Put a cross in the box next to the correct answer. **(1 mark)**

☐ **A** 11

☐ **B** 8

☐ **C** 10

☐ **D** 18

Atomic number and mass number

1   The diagram below shows the structure of a carbon atom.

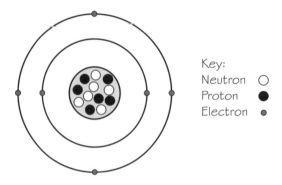

Key:
Neutron ○
Proton ●
Electron •

   (a) What is the atomic number of carbon?   **(1 mark)**

   ....

   (b) What is the charge on a carbon atom?   **(1 mark)**

   ....

2   Oxygen is shown in the periodic table as:

$$^{16}_{8}\text{O}$$

   (a) What does the number 16 represent?   **(1 mark)**

   ....

   (b) What does the number 8 represent?   **(1 mark)**

   ....

3   The element neon has an atomic number of 10 and a mass number of 20.

   (a) How many protons are present in a neon atom?   **(1 mark)**

   ....

   (b) How many neutrons are present in a neon atom?   **(1 mark)**

   ....

   (c) How many electrons are present in a neon atom?   **(1 mark)**

   ....

The periodic table 1

1 Complete the sentence by putting a cross in the box next to the correct answer.

The periodic table arranges elements in order of their: **(1 mark)**

☐ **A** mass number ☐ **B** boiling point

☐ **C** atomic number ☐ **D** cost

2 The images A and B show parts of the periodic table.

    A   B

Li		B	C	N	O	F
Na						
K						
Rb						
Cs						

(a) The elements in image A are arranged in a column.

What are these columns called? **(1 mark)**

....

(b) The elements in image B are arranged in a row.

What are these rows called? **(1 mark)**

....

> **Guided**

(c) Describe the similarities between elements that are placed in vertical columns. **(1 mark)**

Elements in vertical columns have ....

....

3 Complete the sentence by putting a cross in the box next to the correct answer.

The total of the number of protons and neutrons in the nucleus of an atom is called the: **(1 mark)**

☐ **A** atomic number ☐ **B** atomic mass

☐ **C** atomic weight ☐ **D** mass number

> **Guided**

4 Describe how the elements are arranged in the periodic table. **(5 marks)**

The elements are arranged in rows in order of ....

....

These are placed in order of increasing ....

The elements are also arranged into one of ....

....

The elements are also arranged so that the left-hand side of the periodic table are all

....

and then a zig zag line ....

....

Had a go ☐   Nearly there ☐   Nailed it! ☐

The periodic table 2

| | | | | | | | | | | | | | | | | | H | | | | | | | | | | | | | | | | | He |

Li	A												B	B	N	O	F	Ne
Na	Ma												Al	Si	P	C	Cl	D
K	E	Sc	Ti	V	Cr	Mn	Fe	Co	Ni	F	Zn	Ga	Ce	As	Se	G	Kr

1   Identify the missing elements in the periodic table above.   **(7 marks)**

A   ....

B   ....

C   ....

D   ....

E   ....

F   ....

G   ....

2   Identify the names of the elements with the following symbols:

(i)   Li .... (1 mark)

(ii) Na .... (1 mark)

(iii) O .... (1 mark)

(iv) Zn .... (1 mark)

(v) H .... (1 mark)

Isotopes and relative atomic mass

1 Complete the sentence by putting a cross in the box next to the correct answer.

   An isotope is an element with different numbers of: **(1 mark)**

   ☐ **A** electrons

   ☐ **B** protons

   ☐ **C** neutrons

   ☐ **D** electron shells

> **Guided**

2 Describe relative atomic mass. **(2 marks)**

   The relative atomic mass of an element is the .... of a large number

   of atoms of the element and ....

   ....

The atomic number is the smallest number. This number shows how many protons an atom contains.	To calculate the relative atomic mass you need to know the mass numbers of the isotopes present and their percentage abundances.

3 Boron has an atomic number of 5. It has two isotopes, boron-10 and boron-11. The percentage abundances are 20% boron-10 and 80% boron-11.

   (a) How many protons does boron have? **(1 mark)**

   ....

> **Guided**

   (b) Calculate the relative atomic mass of boron. **(2 marks)**

   $[(20 \times 10) + (80 \times 11)]/100$

   = ...

   To find the relative atomic mass from different isotopes you need to use the equation:

   $$[(\text{mass number of isotope } 1 \times \% \text{ abundance}) + (\text{mass number of isotope } 2 \times \% \text{ abundance})]$$

   $100 = $ relative atomic mass

Filling electron shells 1

1　Complete the sentence by putting a cross in the box next to the correct answer.

An atom with the atomic number of 10 has the electron configuration: **(1 mark)**

☐ **A** 2.7　　　☐ **B** 8.2　　　☐ **C** 2.8　　　☐ **D** 2.7.1

2　Which diagram is correct to show the electron shells for sulfur which has 16 electrons?

Put a cross in the box next to the correct answer. **(1 mark)**

☐ **A**　　　☐ **B**　　　☐ **C**　　　☐ **D**

3　This is how phosphorus is shown in the periodic table:

$$^{31}_{15}\text{P}$$

The diagram below shows the electron shells of a phosphorus atom.

(a) Complete the diagram to show the electron
configuration of the phosphorus atom. **(2 marks)**

Use X to represent an electron.

> The first electron shell is closest to the nucleus and can only hold 2 electrons.
>
> The second and third electron shell hold up to 8 electrons.
>
> The fourth electron shell holds any more electrons.

(b) Write the electron configuration for phosphorus. **(1 mark)**

....

4　This is how magnesium is shown in the periodic table:

$$^{24}_{12}\text{Mg}$$

(a) Complete the diagram to show the electron configuration of the magnesium atom.

(2 marks)

Use X to represent an electron.

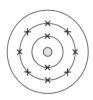

(b) Write the electron configuration for magnesium. **(1 mark)**

....

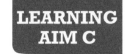

Filling electron shells 2

1 This is how calcium is shown on the periodic table.

$^{40}_{20}Ca$

(a) Complete the diagram to show the electron configuration of the calcium atom. **(2 marks)**

Use X to represent an electron.

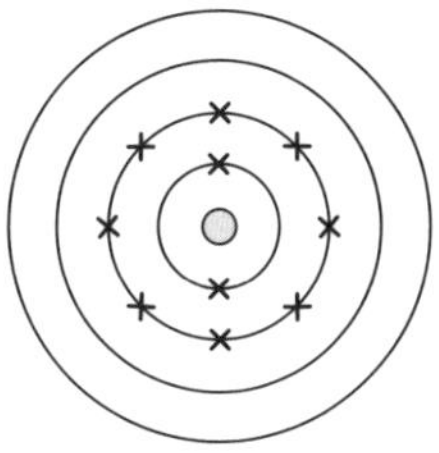

(b) Write the electron configuration for calcium. **(1 mark)**

....

							1 H 1										4 He 2
7 Li 3	9 Be 4											11 B 5	12 C 6	14 N 7	16 O 8	19 F 9	20 Ne 10
23 Na 11	24 Mg 12											27 Al 13	28 Si 14	29 P 15	31 S 16	35.5 Cl 17	40 Ar 18
39 K 19	40 Ca 20	45 Sc 21	48 Ti 22	51 V 23	52 Cr 24	55 Mn 25	56 Fe 26	59 Co 27	59 Ni 28	63.5 Cu 29	65 Zn 30	70 Ga 31	73 Ge 32	75 As 33	79 Se 34	80 Br 35	84 Kr 36

2 Using the periodic table above, draw the electron shells for the following elements.

(a) Li **(1 mark)** **(b)** Mg **(1 mark)**

(c) N **(1 mark)** **(d)** S **(1 mark)**

(e) F **(1 mark)** **(f)** Ne **(1 mark)**

3 Write the electron configuration for the following elements.

(a) Be .... **(1 mark)** **(b)** He .... **(1 mark)**

(c) Ca .... **(1 mark)** **(d)** Na .... **(1 mark)**

(e) Si .... **(1 mark)** **(f)** Ar .... **(1 mark)**

Electron shells and groups

1 Complete the sentence by putting a cross in the box next to the correct answer.

In the periodic table, elements that have the same number of electrons in their outer shell are in the same: **(1 mark)**

☐ **A** row

☐ **B** period

☐ **C** group

☐ **D** section

2 (a) The elements helium, neon and argon are all in Group 0 in the periodic table.

Give **two** reasons why these elements are placed in the same group. **(2 marks)**

1 They all have similar properties to each other.

2 They all have complete ....

(a) Complete the table to show the atomic number and electronic structure of the first three elements in Group 1 in the periodic table. **(6 marks)**

Group 1	Atomic number	Electronic configuration
$^{7}_{3}Li$		
$^{23}_{11}Na$		
$^{39}_{19}K$		

> The atomic number is the number of protons, which is the same as the number of electrons.

3 (a) If an element has six electrons in its outer shell, which group in the periodic table will it be in? **(1 mark)**

....

(b) If an element has five electrons in its outer shell, which group in the periodic table will it be in? **(1 mark)**

....

Metals and non-metals

1 The diagram below shows a simplified version of the periodic table, which includes some but not all of the elements.

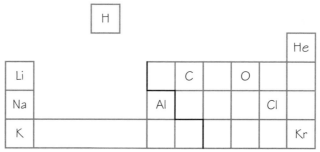

(a) Which **one** of the following elements is a metal? **(1 mark)**

Put a cross in the box next to the correct answer.

☐ **A** Al

☐ **B** O

☐ **C** He

☐ **D** Kr

(b) Which **one** of the following elements is a non-metal? **(1 mark)**

Put a cross in the box next to the correct answer.

☐ **A** Li

☐ **B** K

☐ **C** Cl

☐ **D** Al

> Guided

2 The periodic table can be divided into metals and non-metals.

Explain how you can tell whether an element is a metal or a non-metal from its position in the periodic table. **(1 mark)**

Non-metals appear on the right-hand side of the periodic table. ....

....

....

Compounds and formulae

1   Use the periodic table to help you to answer this question.

    (a) Identify the name of the element from the symbols.   **(3 marks)**

       Li ....

       Na ....

       C ....

    (b) Identify the symbols for each of the elements below.   **(3 marks)**

       Hydrogen ....

       Potassium ....

       Copper ....

2   **(a)** How many sulfur atoms are there in the formula H_2SO_4?   **(1 mark)**

> When there is no number before or after an atom it means that there is one atom present.

       ....

       ....

    (b) How many oxygen atoms are there in the formula $2CO_2$?   **(1 mark)**

       ....

3   Complete the table to show the name and number of atoms in the compound with the formula $Ca(NO_3)_2$.   **(3 marks)**

Atom name	Number of atoms
	1
nitrogen	
oxygen	

Elements, compounds and mixtures

1   Complete the sentence by putting a cross in the box next to the correct answer.

An element is made up of: **(1 mark)**

☐   **A**   92 different types of atom

☐   **B**   1 type of atom

☐   **C**   1 type of compound

☐   **D**   a mixture of atoms

> A molecule is when two or more atoms are bonded together. The atoms that are bonded can be of the same element such as O_2 or different atoms such as CO_2.

2   Oxygen and nitrogen usually exist as molecules.

(a)   Name another molecule. **(1 mark)**

....

(b)   Describe what a molecule is. **(1 mark)**

....

> **Guided**

3   Sea water is a mixture of salt and water. One of the salts in sea water is a compound of sodium and chlorine.

Explain the difference between a mixture and a compound? **(4 marks)**

A mixture contains a number of different substances that are ....

This means that mixtures can be quite easily split up into ....

A compound contains two or more different types of atom that are ....

.... They can only be split ....

....

Word equations

1   In a chemical reaction, substances react to produce new substances.

    (a)   Give the definition of the following substances in a chemical reaction:

       (i)   reactants   **(1 mark)**

       ....

       (ii)   product   **(1 mark)**

       ....

    (b)   Write the word equation for the reaction of carbon and a molecule of oxygen.   **(1 mark)**

       ....

    (c)   Write the word equation for the reaction of hydrogen and a molecule of water.   **(1 mark)**

       ....

2   Complete the sentence by putting a cross in the box next to the correct answer.

    In a chemical reaction the atoms involved are: **(1 mark)**

       ☐   **A**   created and some are destroyed

       ☐   **B**   neither created nor destroyed

       ☐   **C**   not created but some are destroyed

       ☐   **D**   destroyed

3   Complete the word equations for the reactions shown below.

    (a)   zinc + hydrochloric acid → .... + water + hydrogen   **(1 mark)**

    (b)   sodium hydroxide + hydrochloric acid → .... + water   **(1 mark)**

    (c)   iron + ... → iron chloride + hydrogen   **(1 mark)**

    (d)   magnesium + sulfuric acid → .... + hydrogen   **(1 mark)**

Balanced chemical equations

1   Balance the following equations:

   (a) $Mg + ... HCl \rightarrow MgCl_2 + H_2$ **(1 mark)**

   (b) $CuO + ... HCl \rightarrow CuCl_2 + H_2O$ **(1 mark)**

   (c) $H_2SO_4 + ... NaOH \rightarrow Na_2SO_4 + ... H_2O$ **(2 marks)**

2   Write balanced equations for the following reactions:

   (a)   nitric acid and zinc oxide

   .... **(1 mark)**

   (b)   hydrochloric acid and copper carbonate

   .... **(1 mark)**

   (c)   sulfuric acid and sodium hydroxide

   .... **(1 mark)**

3   Which **one** of the following equations for the reaction between zinc and nitric acid is balanced?   **(1 mark)**

   Put a cross in the box next to the correct answer.

   ☐   **A** $Zn + 2HNO_3 \rightarrow ZnNO_3 + H_2$

   ☐   **B** $Zn + 2HNO_3 \rightarrow Zn(NO_3)_2 + H_2$

   ☐   **C** $Zn + HNO_3 \rightarrow Zn(NO_3)_3 + H_2$

   ☐   **D** $Zn + HNO_3 \rightarrow ZnNO_3 + H_2$

4   Complete the table below with the correct number of each atom in the formula $Zn(NO_3)_2$.   **(3 marks)**

Atom	Number
Zn	
N	
O	

Acids, bases and alkalis

1   What is the pH of an acid?

Put a cross in the box next to the correct answer.   **(1 mark)**

☐ **A** more than 7   ☐ **B** 7   ☐ **C** less than 7   ☐ **D** 14

2   Complete the sentence by putting a cross in the box next to the correct answer.

When blue litmus paper is added to an acid, the litmus paper turns: **(1 mark)**

☐ **A** red   ☐ **B** green   ☐ **C** purple   ☐ **D** blue

3   A student uses universal indicator to find out the pH of three different substances.

The solution in test tube A turned purple.

The solution in test tube B turned yellow/green.

The solution in test tube C turned orange.

Identify the substances as either acid, alkali or neutral.   **(3 marks)**

A   ....

B   ....

C   ....

4   A base is a substance that can react with an acid to neutralise it.

   (a) Name a base.   **(1 mark)**

   ┌───┐
   │ Zinc oxide and sodium hydroxide are   │
   │ bases. Can you think of any others?   │
   └───┘

   ....

> **Guided**   **(b)** Describe the difference between a base and an alkali.   **(2 marks)**

   Most bases will not dissolve in water. An alkali is a type of base that ....

   ....

Neutralisation reactions

1 What substance needs to be added to an acid to neutralise it?
Put a cross in the box next to the correct answer.   **(1 mark)**

☐ **A** water   ☐ **B** base   ☐ **C** hydrogen   ☐ **D** salt

2 **(a)** Complete the word equation for the reaction of an acid and a base.   **(2 marks)**

acid + base → ....

(b) Complete the word equation for the reaction of nitric acid and sodium hydroxide.   **(2 marks)**

nitric acid + sodium hydroxide → ....

> Remember, the salt formed from a reaction of nitric acid with a base is always a nitrate salt.

> Guided

3 When a base is added to an acid, a neutralisation reaction occurs.
Explain what happens if incorrect quantities of an acid or a base are added in a neutralisation reaction.   **(2 marks)**

If too much acid or base is added there will be no neutralisation reaction, as too much acid

will mean that the product remains .... or, if too

much base is added the product will remain ....

4 **(a)** Which of the following substances is a salt?
Put a cross in the box next to the correct answer.   **(1 mark)**

☐ **A** sulfuric acid   ☐ **B** copper chloride

☐ **C** copper oxide   ☐ **D** sodium hydroxide

(b) Which of the following substances is a base?
Put a cross in the box next to the correct answer.   **(1 mark)**

☐ **A** sodium nitrate   ☐ **B** nitric acid

☐ **C** copper sulfate   ☐ **D** sodium hydroxide

5 When copper oxide and an acid are added together a neutralisation reaction occurs.

(a) Name the two products that are always formed in a neutralisation reaction.   **(2 marks)**

....

....

....

> When naming salts the name of the base gives the first part of the name and the acid gives the second part of the name.

(b) Complete the word equations for the following reactions.

(i) zinc oxide + hydrochloric acid → .... + ... **(1 mark)**

(ii) copper oxide + ... → copper nitrate + ... **(1 mark)**

(iii) copper oxide + sulfuric acid → .... + ... **(1 mark)**

Equations for neutralisation reactions

1   The reaction between nitric acid and sodium hydroxide is a neutralisation reaction.
    Complete a word equation for this reaction.   **(2 marks)**

    ....

    ....

2   When copper oxide is reacted with an acid, a neutralisation reaction occurs.

    (a) Name the two products that are always formed in a neutralisation reaction.   **(2 marks)**

    ....

    ....

    (b) Complete the word equations for these neutralisation reactions.

    Guided   **(i)**   copper oxide + hydrochloric acid → copper chloride + water   **(1 mark)**

    (ii) copper oxide + ... → copper nitrate + ... **(1 mark)**

    (iii) copper oxide + sulfuric acid → .... + ... **(1 mark)**

    > When naming salts the first part of the name comes from the base gives and the second part of the name comes from the acid.

3   In a neutralisation reaction, describe what will happen to the pH of an acid
    solution when an alkali is added.   **(2 marks)**

    ....

    ....

Reactions of acids with metals

1   Complete the word equation for the reaction of an acid with a metal.   **(2 marks)**

    acid + metal → .... + ...

2   Complete the sentence by putting a cross in the box next to the correct answer.

    In the reaction of sulfuric acid and calcium one of the products formed is: **(1 mark)**

    ☐   **A**   calcium sulfate

    ☐   **B**   calcium oxide

    ☐   **C**   calcium nitrate

    ☐   **D**   calcium acid

3   Complete the word equations for the following reactions.

    (a) zinc + hydrochloric acid → .... + ... **(1 mark)**

    (b) magnesium + ... → magnesium sulfate + ... **(1 mark)**

    (c) iron + hydrochloric acid → .... + ... **(1 mark)**

4   State the names of the salts produced when the following acids are added to a metal:

    (a) hydrochloric acid   **(1 mark)**

    ....

    (b) sulfuric acid   **(1 mark)**

    ....

    (c) nitric acid   **(1 mark)**

    ....

Reactions of acids with carbonates

1 A metal carbonate will react with an acid to form three products.

   What are the three products formed? **(3 marks)**

   1 ....

   2 ....

   3 ....

2 A student adds some calcium carbonate to sulfuric acid.

   Describe how the student can see that a gas has been produced in the reaction.

   (1 mark)

   ....

   ....

   ....

   > The question is asking how a person can tell from observing the experiment so you need to think about what you might see if you were watching this experiment.

3 Complete the word equations for the following reactions.

   (a) sulfuric acid + sodium carbonate → .... +

   .... + ... **(1 mark)**

   (b) hydrochloric acid + copper carbonate → .... +

   .... + ... **(1 mark)**

   (c) nitric acid + calcium carbonate → .... +

   .... + ... **(1 mark)**

Tests for hydrogen and carbon dioxide

1 Complete the sentences by putting a cross in the box next to the correct answer.

   (a) One of the products in the reaction between an acid and a metal is: **(1 mark)**

   ☐ **A** carbon dioxide

   ☐ **B** hydrogen

   ☐ **C** oxygen

   ☐ **D** a hydroxide

   (b) One of the products in the reaction between an acid and a carbonate is: **(1 mark)**

   ☐ **A** carbon dioxide

   ☐ **B** hydrogen

   ☐ **C** oxygen

   ☐ **D** an oxide

▷ **Guided** ▷ 2 The diagram below shows an acid and a carbonate reacting together in a test tube.

Reacting
substances

Limewater

Explain why the test tube with the reacting substances contains a tube leading to
another test tube containing limewater.   **(1 mark)**

The reaction between an acid and a carbonate produces ....

This gas goes into the limewater and is bubbled through it. If the limewater ....

....

▷ **Guided** ▷ 3 When an acid and metal are added together one of the products is a gas.

Describe what experiment you would carry out to test what gas has been produced.   **(2 marks)**

An acid and a metal react to produce .... To test if

this gas has been produced ....

....

....

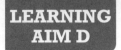

Hazard symbols

1 Identify each of the following hazard symbols. **(5 marks)**

(a)

....

(b)

....

(c)

....

(d)

....

(e)

....

2 Explain why hazard symbols are used rather than written information on the chemical container stating the hazards associated with the chemical. **(3 marks)**

....

....

....

3 **(a)** A substance has the corrosive hazard symbol on its container. What precautions do you need to take when using this substance? **(1 mark)**

....

....

(b) Give an example of a type of substance which may have the corrosive symbol on its container. **(1 mark)**

....

Applications of neutralisation reactions

1 Which **one** of the following would be the best substance to help to relieve the symptoms of indigestion?

Put a cross in the box next to the correct answer.   **(1 mark)**

☐ **A** water

☐ **B** magnesium carbonate

☐ **C** dilute hydrochloric acid

☐ **D** carbon dioxide

> Indigestion is caused from too much acid so the substance will need to be a base or a carbonate to neutralise the excess acid.

2 Acid rain can have a negative affect on the environment.

Explain how acid rain can lead to damage of the environment and how this damage can be reduced.   **(6 marks)**

Acid rain

....

....

....

....

....

....

....

....

> Your explanation should include the following:
> - The acid rain makes lakes acidic which kills the fish in those lakes. It can also kill trees and plants and erode stonework.
> - To reduce the damage caused by acid rain, alkaline substances such as lime or calcium carbonate can be used and added to the lakes to neutralise the acid.

....

....

....

....

....

Learning aim D: 6-mark questions 1

1   Sand in water is an example of a mixture of substances. Iron sulfate is an example of a compound.

Explain the differences and similarities between a compound and a mixture.   **(6 marks)**

> You will be more successful in extended writing questions if you plan your answer before you start writing. When answering this question, you will need to think about the following:
>
> - What has happened to the elements contained in a compound?
> - How easily can you split out the substances contained in a mixture?

....

....

....

....

....

....

....

....

....

....

....

....

....

....

....

....

....

....

....

....

....

Learning aim D: 6-mark questions 2

1 When a scientist is writing chemical equations it is important that the equation is balanced.

Explain how the following equation can be balanced:

$Mg + HCl \rightarrow MgCl_2 + H_2$ (6 marks)

....

....

....

....

....

....

....

....

....

....

....

....

....

....

....

....

....

....

....

....

....

....

....

Balanced equations for reactions with acids

1 Write balanced equations for the following reactions.

(a) HNO_3 + $CaCO_3 \rightarrow$ .... (1 mark)

(b) H_2SO_4 + $CaCO_3 \rightarrow$ .... (1 mark)

(c) HCl + $CaCO_3 \rightarrow$ .... (1 mark)

(d) H_2SO_4 + $Na_2CO_3 \rightarrow$ .... (1 mark)

(e) HCl + $Na_2CO_3 \rightarrow$ .... (1 mark)

(f) H_2SO_4 + $NaOH \rightarrow$ .... (1 mark)

(g) CuO + $HCl \rightarrow$ .... (1 mark)

(h) Mg + $HCl \rightarrow$ .... (1 mark)

(i) Ca + $H_2SO_4 \rightarrow$ .... (1 mark)

(j) Zn + $2HNO_3 \rightarrow$ .... (1 mark)

(k) ZnO + $HNO_3 \rightarrow$ .... (1 mark)

Forms of energy

1 There are many different types of energy. Name the type of energy generated by the following objects:

(a)

.... **(1 mark)**

(b)

.... **(1 mark)**

(c)

.... **(1 mark)**

> **Guided**

2 Describe the different types of energy used and produced by a vacuum cleaner.   **(3 marks)**

A vacuum cleaner uses electrical energy to produce .... energy to

suck up the dust from carpets. It also produces ....

when it is in use.

3 Describe the differences between solar energy and light energy.   **(2 marks)**

....

....

....

> Think about the sources of
> these forms of energy.

Uses of energy

1 People use lots of different types of energy for everyday tasks in their homes.

Give one example of each of these types of energy.

(a) thermal energy

.... **(1 mark)**

(b) mechanical energy

.... **(1 mark)**

(c) sound

.... **(1 mark)**

2 In a game of tennis, several different types of energy are used and transformed.

In a tennis serve, the server throws the ball up into the air and then hits the ball as it comes down from the throw.

(a) Which type of energy does the tennis ball show when it is travelling up into the air?

(1 mark)

> The ball is moving so it is a type of movement energy.

....

(b) Which type of energy does the tennis ball show when it has reached the highest point of the throw? **(1 mark)**

> At the top of the throw the ball is not moving.

....

3 Complete the flow chart to show the energy transformation from when a tennis player eats food to them moving around the tennis court to play tennis. **(1 mark)**

| Chemical energy | → | .... energy |

Energy stores

1 Which **one** of the following is a form of stored energy?

   Put a cross in the box next to the correct answer.   **(1 mark)**

   ☐ **A** electrical energy

   ☐ **B** sound energy

   ☐ **C** potential energy

   ☐ **D** light energy

> Guided

2 Batteries are often used to power toys. Explain how batteries supply this
   energy.   **(2 marks)**

   Batteries store ....:........ which can

   be transferred into .... to power

   the toys.

   > You need to explain the type
   > of energy that batteries store
   > and the type of energy they
   > give out.

3 In a game of squash, players use rackets to hit the ball against the squash court walls.

   Identify the different types of energy in the racket shown in images A and B.   **(2 marks)**

   A   B

   A   The ball presses back into the racket head.

   ....

   B   The ball is hit and moves away from the racket head.

   ....

Thermal energy transfers

1 Complete the sentences by putting a cross in the box next to the correct answer.

  (a) The transfer of thermal energy through the contact of objects is called: **(1 mark)**

    ☐ **A** convection

    ☐ **B** conduction

    ☐ **C** radiation

    ☐ **D** evaporation

  (b) Radiation transfers thermal energy through: **(1 mark)**

    ☐ **A** fluids

    ☐ **B** a vacuum

    ☐ **C** direct contact

    ☐ **D** wind

Guided 2 (a) Explain why saucepans are usually made of a metal. **(3 marks)**

    Heat is transferred from the hob to the saucepan by

    ....

    Metal is a .... of heat which means ....

    ....

  (b) Suggest one reason why a saucepan handle might be made of wood. **(2 marks)**

    ....

    ....

> Think about the properties of wood: how well does it conduct heat?

    ....

  (c) When soup is heated in a saucepan, thermal energy transfers by convection.

    Describe the transfer of thermal energy by convection in a fluid. **(3 marks)**

    ....

    ....

    ....

Measuring energy

1 Complete the sentence by putting a cross in the box next to the correct answer.

Energy transfer is measured in: **(1 mark)**

☐ **A** minutes   ☐ **B** newtons

☐ **C** joules   ☐ **D** pounds

2 The diagram opposite shows energy transfer in a television set.

(a) How many joules of energy are wasted? **(1 mark)**

....

....

Energy supplied = 40 J

Heat energy = 20 J

Light energy = 15 J

Sound energy = 5 J

> Think about which of the three types of energy produced is not required for a TV to function.

> **Guided**

(b) $\text{efficiency} = \dfrac{\text{useful energy transferred by the device}}{\text{total energy supplied to the device}} \times 100\%$

Calculate the efficiency of the television. **(2 marks)**

$$\text{efficiency} = \frac{15 + 5}{40} \times 100$$

$$= \text{......................} \%$$

> Substitute the values into the equation for efficiency.

> **Guided**

(c) A new plasma television has been designed that uses less power than a liquid crystal (LC) television.

The table shows how the two televisions compare.

	LC TV	New Plasma TV
Power consumption	40	10 W
Expected life	5000 hours	20 000 hours
Price	£800	£1500

Identify the television you think will sell the most and explain why.

Use a calculation to justify your answer. **(4 marks)**

People would buy the new plasma television because it ....

.... and ....

which offsets the higher price when compared with the LC TV.

$\dfrac{(800/5000)}{(1500/20\,000)} = \dfrac{0.16}{0.075} =$ .... times more cost-effective

....

Power

1 Complete the sentence by putting a cross in the box next to the correct answer.

Power is measured in: **(1 mark)**

☐ **A** joules

☐ **B** seconds

☐ **C** watts

☐ **D** volts

2 Power (watts) = $\dfrac{\text{energy (joules)}}{\text{time (seconds)}}$

> **Guided**

(a) Calculate the power of a light bulb that transfers 55 000 J in 15 minutes? **(3 marks)**

15 minutes = 900 seconds

Power $= \dfrac{55\,000}{900}$

> Work out the time in seconds first, then substitute the values into the power equation.

= .... W

(b) An energy saving light bulb is rated as 25 W.

Calculate how much energy is transferred in 5 seconds. **(3 marks)**

> You need to be able to use the equation for power to work out energy and time as well as power.

....

....

....

3 Explain why a person will use more power when running 1 km on a treadmill than walking the same distance on the same treadmill. **(2 marks)**

> Think about what power is before you attempt to answer this question.

....

....

Paying for electricity

1 The image shows the readings on a household electricity meter at 9 o'clock on Monday morning and 9 o'clock on Monday evening.

0 9 6 8 5   **0 9 7 2 0**
9 am   9 pm

> **Guided**

(a) Calculate the amount of electricity (in kilowatt hour) used during this 12-hour period.   **(1 mark)**

09720 – 09685 = ... kWh

> Subtract the starting reading from the finishing reading.

Each kilowatt hour (kWh) of electricity costs 8 pence.

(b) Calculate the cost of the electricity used in this 12-hour period.   **(1 mark)**

....

> Use your answer for part (a) and multiply it by the cost per unit. Always set your calculation out clearly as credit is given for the method.

> **Guided**

(c) On Tuesday morning, a 9 kW heater was used for 3 hours. Calculate how much energy was transferred by the heater.   **(1 mark)**

energy transferred (kWh) = power (kW) x time (h)

....

> **Guided**

2 A school wants to reduce its electricity costs and is deciding whether to install a slow heating low power heater or a faster heating high power heater.

> Convert the power rating for the low power heater into kW before calculating the cost of electricity.

The table below compares the two heaters.

	Low power heater	Higher power heater
Power	900 W	2 kW
Number of hours required per week	40	30

The school pays 12p per KWh for its electricity.

Explain which heater you think the school should buy.

Use calculations to justify your answer.   **(5 marks)**

The weekly power consumption of the low power heater is: 0.9 x 40 = 36 kWh

Therefore the weekly cost of the low power heater is 36 x 0.12 = ...

The weekly power consumption of the high power heater is: ....

Therefore the weekly cost of the high power heater is: ....

Conclusion: ....

....

....

Efficiency of energy transfers

1 **(a)** Describe what is meant by an efficient energy transfer. **(1 mark)**

....

(b) Explain why energy is lost during an energy transfer. **(1 mark)**

....

> When energy is transferred some energy will always be wasted. Wasted energy is where some of the energy that is transferred into a form of energy that is not useful.

2 Identify the energy transfers that occur in the following appliances:

(a) electrical energy to a kettle **(2 marks)**

....

....

(b) electrical energy to a light **(2 marks)**

....

....

(c) a book falling off a shelf **(4 marks)**

....

....

....

....

3 The efficiency of an energy transfer can be worked out using the equation:

(useful energy transferred ÷ energy supplied) × 100 = efficiency

Calculate the efficiency of the following energy transfers:

(a) an electric drill transfers 800 J of electrical energy into 350 J of kinetic energy **(1 mark)**

....

(b) a light bulb transfers 50 J of electrical energy into 30 J of light energy **(1 mark)**

....

(c) a television transfers 1000 J of electrical energy into 600 J of sound and light
energy **(1 mark)**

....

(d) a kettle transfers 400 J of electrical energy into 250 J of thermal energy **(1 mark)**

....

Renewable energy resources

1 Explain what is meant by 'renewable energy resources'. **(2 marks)**

....

....

2 Complete the sentence by putting a cross in the box next to the correct answer.

The best energy source to power a calculator is: **(1 mark)**

☐ **A** nuclear energy ☐ **B** solar energy ☐ **C** tidal energy ☐ **D** wind energy

3 Describe how the following renewable energy resources produce electricity.

Guided

(a) Wind: Wind turbines transform .... of the wind

directly into electrical energy. **(1 mark)**

(b) Hydroelectric power: ....

.... **(1 mark)**

(c) Tidal: ....

.... **(1 mark)**

4 Fitting solar panels to house roofs is becoming increasingly common.

Explain the environmental benefits of solar power. **(2 marks)**

....

....

....

> The question asks about environmental benefits, so there is no need to mention disadvantages or financial cost.

Guided

5 Describe the advantages of hydroelectric power stations over coal power stations. **(3 marks)**

Hydroelectric power stations use ...., and do not

produce any pollution such as sulfur or carbon dioxide. The running costs ....

....

....

Non-renewable energy resources

> **Guided**

1 Explain what is meant by 'non-renewable energy resources'. **(2 marks)**

This means that once the energy resource has been used up ....

....

2 A nuclear power station uses non-renewable energy resources to produce electricity.

(a) Complete the sentences by putting a cross in the box next to the correct answers.

   (i) The turbine in a nuclear power station is driven by: **(1 mark)**

     ☐ **A** steam   ☐ **B** electricity

     ☐ **C** electrons   ☐ **D** conduction

   (ii) The turbine transfers .... energy to the generator. **(1 mark)**

     ☐ **A** potential ☐ **B** kinetic

     ☐ **C** elastic   ☐ **D** thermal

(b) Describe the disadvantages of nuclear energy. **(3 marks)**

....

....

....

....

> Think about the waste products: what has to happen to them and how much does it cost? What if something goes wrong?

3 The table shows the costs associated with providing domestic electricity from one form of renewable energy and one form of non-renewable electricity.

	Set up cost	Fuel cost
Solar power	£1000	0p
Gas	£250	30p

> Compare the set up costs, fuel costs, environmental costs and reliability.

Compare the two methods. **(4 marks)**

....

....

....

....

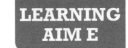

Using energy effectively

1 Identify **three** ways in which it is possible to reduce use of electrical energy in the home. **(3 marks)**

....

....

....

2 Other than to reduce costs, explain why it is important for businesses and homes to reduce their use of electrical energy. **(2 marks)**

....

....

3 Describe what is meant by the principle 'energy cannot be created or destroyed'. **(3 marks)**

....

....

....

4 What is the unit of energy?

Put a cross in the box next to the correct statement

☐ **A** hertz

☐ **B** joules

☐ **C** kilograms

☐ **D** metres per second

Learning aim E: 6-mark questions 1

1   Energy can exist in many different forms and has many different uses. Energy can also be transformed to different types of energy.

At a fairground, a rollercoaster ride provides examples of many different types of energy. Discuss the different types of energy transfer that occur on a roller coaster ride.

You may use drawings to illustrate your answer.   **(6 marks)**

> You will be more successful in extended writing questions if you plan your answer before you start writing. When answering this question, you will need to think about the following:
>
> • What are the different types of energy that could be included in a rollercoaster ride?
> • Explain what each type of energy is, to show your understanding of these concepts.
> • Remember that energy cannot be created or destroyed, so always refer to energy being transferred.
>
> It is always a good idea to include a drawing if the question suggests that they can be included. This will not only demonstrate your understanding of the subject area, but it will also give you some ideas on how to answer the question and help you to structure your answer.

Learning aim E: 6-mark questions 2

1   Simon wants to hire a laptop computer. He has selected two possible types of laptop and the details of each are shown in the table below. Simon wants to keep his costs as low as possible. He pays 19p per kilowatt per hour for electricity and he will be using the laptop for 8 hours a day for 300 days in total.

Laptop	A	B
Hire cost per laptop	£255	£265
Watts	45	20

Use calculations to explain which laptop you think would be the most suitable for Simon.

energy transferred (kWh) = power (kW) × time (h)   **(6 marks)**

> You will be more successful in extended writing questions if you plan your answer before you start writing. When answering this question, you will need to think about the following:
>
> - How much is the cost of running each computer?
> - What is the cost of electricity used by each computer in one day?
> - If the equation uses kW units for power, you will need to convert W to kW.
> - How do you use the values that you have calculated to justify which lap top is the better one for Simon to buy?
>
> Remember that you need to show your workings so that the method you are using to carry out each calculation is clear.

....

....

....

....

....

....

....

....

....

....

....

Wave characteristics

1 (a) Most waves have the following structure.

Label the diagram to show the following parts of the wave:

(i) amplitude   (1 mark)

(ii) wavelength   (1 mark)

(b) The diagrams below show three waves with different frequencies.

A   B   C

(i) Identify the wave with the highest frequency.   (1 mark)

....

> You will need to know and be able to use the terms amplitude, wavelength and frequency and know the units for each.

(ii) Complete the sentence by putting a cross in the box next to the correct answer.

Frequency of waves is measured in: (1 mark)

☐ A watts

☐ B hertz

☐ C joules

☐ D metres per second

Guided 2 (a) Define the term 'wavelength'.   (1 mark)

Wavelength is the distance from the .... of one wave to the .... of the next wave.

> You should use appropriate terminology when you define scientific terms.

(b) What is the unit of wavelength?   (1 mark)

....

Wave calculations

1   Complete the sentence by putting a cross in the box next to the correct answer.

The amplitude of a wave: **(1 mark)**

☐   **A**   increases wavelength

☐   **B**   decreases wavelength

☐   **C**   does not affect wavelength

☐   **D**   is measured from the top to the bottom of a wave

> **Guided**

2   The diagram shows a wave.

Use the equation:

   wave speed (m/s) = frequency (Hz) × wavelength (m)

to calculate:

(a)   The speed of a wave with a frequency 10 Hz and a
       wavelength 50 metres.   **(1 mark)**

   ....

> Always include the units in your
> answer.

(b)   The frequency of a wave with a wave speed of 300 m/s and a wavelength
       of 30 m.   **(2 marks)**

   Frequency = wave speed / wavelength

> Rearrange the equation first – formula
> triangles will help.

   ....

   ....

(c)   The wavelength of a wave with a wave speed of 500 m/s and a frequency
       of 40 Hz.   **(2 marks)**

   ....

   ....

> **Guided**

3   Which wave has the fastest wave speed? Use calculations to justify your answer.   **(3 marks)**

A   A wave with a frequency of 15 Hz and a wavelength of 10 m.

B   A wave with a frequency of 20 Hz and a wavelength of 15 m.

   wave speed (m/s) = frequency (Hz) x wavelength (m)

   Wave A: wave speed = 15 x 10

                    = ... m/s

   Wave B: wave speed = ...

                    = ... m/s

> First, state which equation
> you need, then calculate
> the speed of each wave.
> Always check to make sure
> you have answered the
> original question.

   .... will have the fastest wave speed.

The electromagnetic spectrum

1   Complete the sentence by putting a cross in the box next to the correct answer.

The electromagnetic spectrum is a range of electromagnetic waves with continuous wavelengths and continuous: **(1 mark)**

☐ **A** frequencies

☐ **B** amplitudes

☐ **C** sizes

☐ **D** speeds

2   What is the frequency of a wave that has a wavelength of 10 m and a wave speed of 80 m/s?   **(2 marks)**

> Frequency = wave speed / wavelength

....

....

Guided

3   Electromagnetic radiation is used in a range of objects for a range of functions.

Identify the type of electromagnetic radiation used in items A–D below.   **(4 marks)**

A ....

B ....

C ....

D ....

> Choose your answers from this list:
> • X-rays   • UV rays   • Radio waves   • Microwaves

4   The electromagnetic spectrum is a range of electromagnetic waves with continuous wavelengths and frequencies.

Complete the table below which shows the different types of electromagnetic wave in order of frequency.

> A mnemonic can help your remember the correct order.

(3 marks)

Radio waves	....	Infrared	....	Ultraviolet	....	Gamma rays

→ Increasing frequency

Radio waves

1 Complete the sentence by putting a cross in the box next to the correct answer.

A mains-operated radio converts: **(1 mark)**

☐ **A** electrical energy into light energy

☐ **B** chemical energy to sound energy

☐ **C** electrical energy into thermal energy

☐ **D** electrical energy into sound energy

2 Radio waves are a form of electromagnetic radiation.

(a) Where in relation to wavelength and wave frequency in the electromagnetic spectrum can radio waves be located?   **(1 mark)**

....

(b) Give two uses of radio waves.   **(2 marks)**

....

....

(c) Explain why radio waves are not harmful to humans.   **(2 marks)**

The higher the frequency of the wave, the...

....

Radio waves have the .... frequency in the electromagnetic spectrum so do

not cause any harm to humans.

(d) Calculate the wave speed of a radio wave with a frequency of 10 Hz and wavelength of 15 m.   **(2 marks)**

wave speed = frequency x wavelength

= 10 x 15

= .... m/s

Microwaves

1 Complete the sentence by putting a cross in the box next to the correct answer.

Microwaves are a type of: **(1 mark)**

☐ **A** infrared radiation

☐ **B** radio wave

☐ **C** ultraviolet radiation

☐ **D** X-ray

2 Microwave ovens are used in many homes to heat food.

(a) Complete the sentence by putting a cross in the box next to the correct answer.

When food absorbs microwaves, the energy from the microwaves is converted into:

☐ **A** potential energy

☐ **B** kinetic energy

☐ **C** light energy

☐ **D** sound energy

> **Guided**

(b) Microwaves used in microwave ovens have a wavelength of 0.125 metres and a frequency of approximately 2400 million hertz.

Calculate their wave speed **(2 marks)**

Wave speed = wavelength x frequency

= .... x 2 400 000 000

= ....

┌───┐
│ Remember to include the units in your answer. │
└───┘

(c) Give two other uses of microwaves. **(2 marks)**

1 ....

2 ....

Infrared radiation

1 Infrared radiation is used for thermal imaging.

What colour are warm objects shown as in infrared imaging?

Put a cross in the box next to the correct answer.   **(1 mark)**

☐ **A** green

☐ **B** blue

☐ **C** red

☐ **D** black

2 **(a)** Infrared radiation is used in ovens and in a television remote control.

Give **three** other uses of infrared radiation.   **(3 marks)**

1 ....

2 ....

3 ....

> **Guided**

(b) Explain why touching the beam of infrared radiation from a television remote
control is harmless but getting too close to an electric grill can cause a burn.   **(3 marks)**

Short infrared waves do not cause any heating, but long infrared waves do. The TV remote

control uses ....

....

Grills use ....

....

Visible light

1 Complete the sentence by putting a cross in the box next to the correct answer.

Visible light is the only part of the electromagnetic spectrum that can: **(1 mark)**

☐ **A** burn the skin

☐ **B** lead to skin cancer

☐ **C** be seen by the human eye

☐ **D** be used as optical fibres

2 Visible light is part of the electromagnetic spectrum.

Complete the table to show all the colours of visible light in order of wavelength. **(5 marks)**

Violet
Red

shortest wavelength
longest wavelength

> The following colours are in visible light:
> - Violet
> - Red
> - Orange
> - Green
> - Blue
> - Indigo
> - Yellow
>
> Use a mnemonic to help you remember the correct order.

3 Describe how visible light is used in photography. **(3 marks)**

....

....

....

....

....

....

Ultraviolet light

1 Put a cross in the box next to the correct statement. **(1 mark)**

☐ **A** Ultraviolet light waves have a higher frequency than gamma rays.

☐ **B** Ultraviolet light waves have a higher frequency than visible light.

☐ **C** Ultraviolet light waves have a lower frequency than microwaves.

☐ **D** Ultraviolet light waves have a lower frequency than radio waves.

2 UV light has many different purposes, for example fluorescent lamps.

Give two further uses of ultraviolet light. **(2 marks)**

1 ....

2 ....

> **Guided**

3 Too much exposure to sunlight can cause harmful effects due to UV light.

Describe the harmful effects of overexposure to ultraviolet light. **(3 marks)**

Excess exposure to UV light can cause sunburn which ....

....

Excess exposure to UV light can also .... and cause

serious eye conditions such as cataracts.

4 Very high levels of ultraviolet light can kill living cells.

Explain why this fact means that ultraviolet light can be used disinfect water. **(2 marks)**

....

....

X-rays

1 Identify **two** uses of X-rays. **(2 marks)**

1 ....

2 ....

2 A device was invented in the 1920s that used X-rays to help to fit children's shoes.

The child placed their foot in the device in their new shoes and the device used X-rays to show how well the shoe fitted the child's foot. The device was initially thought to have no harmful effects but was prohibited in the 1950s.

(a) Identify **two** of the possible harmful effects from this machine. **(2 marks)**

1 ....

2 ....

> **Guided**

(b) Explain why radiographers who use X-ray machines wear lead waistcoats when operating X-ray machines. **(2 marks)**

X-rays have a high frequency that ....

....

Gamma rays

1 (a) Complete the sentences by putting a cross in the box next to the correct answers.

The frequency of gamma rays is: **(1 mark)**

☐ **A** lower than microwaves

☐ **B** the same as X-rays

☐ **C** higher than X-rays

☐ **D** the lowest in the electromagnetic spectrum

(b) The typical wavelength of gamma rays is: **(1 mark)**

☐ **A** 10^{-10} m

☐ **B** 10^{-7} m

☐ **C** 10^{-12} m

☐ **D** 10^{-5} m

2 Gamma rays are used to treat cancer, yet overexposure to gamma rays can cause cancer.

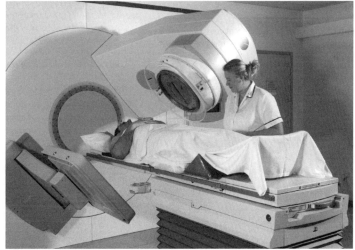

> **Guided**

(a) Explain how gamma rays can both cause and treat cancer. **(3 marks)**

Gamma rays have a very high frequency and therefore carry high energy which means they

can damage or kill living cells. ....

....

(b) Describe what protective clothing a doctor would need to wear to protect
themselves when treating a patient with gamma rays. **(2 marks)**

....

....

Answers

Learning aim A

1. Cell structure and function 1

1 B

2 A – Nucleus.
  B – Cell membrane.
  C – Cytoplasm.

3 A plant cell has three different parts compared to an animal cell. These parts are a cell wall which provides the cell with shape and support, chloroplasts which are where photosynthesis takes place, and vacuoles that are filled with sap and store nutrients.

2. Cell structure and function 2

1 A

2 (a) The nucleus contains genetic information that controls the activities of the cell.
  (b) The cell membrane allows substances to enter and exit the cell.
  (c) The mitochondria are the sites of respiration.

3 The function of the root hair cell is to absorb water and nutrients. The root hair cell has a long extension to give it a larger surface area to maximise absorption.

3. Plant cell organelles

1 Photosynthesis takes place in the chloroplasts which are located in the leaves of the plant.

2 A vacuole is filled with cell sap which stores nutrients; the sap also provides extra support for the cell.

3 (a) Guard cell.
  (b) The function of the guard cells is to open or close a pore or small hole in the leaf to let in carbon dioxide, which is needed for photosynthesis.

4. Animal cell organelles

1 A – Nucleus.
  B – Cell membrane.
  C – Cytoplasm.
  D – Mitochondrion.

2 Plant cells and animal cells both have (*any three of*):
  1 – A cell membrane.
  2 – A nucleus.
  3 – Mitochondria.
  4 – Cytoplasm.

3 (a) The nucleus contains genetic information that controls the activities of the cell.
  (b) The cell membrane controls entry and exit of substances from the cell.
  (c) The cytoplasm is where many chemical reactions essential for life take place.

5. Cells, tissues and organs

1 A

2 An organ system is a group of organs that work together to carry out a particular function in the body.

3 *Example answer:* The cardiovascular system is the body's main transport system which takes oxygen and nutrients to the body cells and takes away waste products.

6. Function of plant organs

1 C

2 B

3 A leaf contains chloroplasts which is where photosynthesis takes place. Leaves are used in plants to produce energy.

4 (a) Transpiration
  (b) Leaves lose water by evaporation from tiny pores in the leaf. This draws water up from the roots to every part of the plant, through the xylem.

7. DNA

1 A

2 (a) 1 Adenine
     2 Thymine
     3 Guanine
     4 Cytosine
  (b) Adenine pairs with thymine. Guanine pairs with cytosine.

3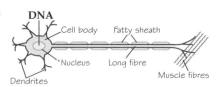

8. Chromosomes and genes

1 C

2 D

3 Genes are short lengths of DNA which give instructions for individual characteristics such as hair colour.

4 (a) The male gamete is the sperm. The female gamete is the egg.
  (b) 23

5 Chromosomes come in pairs as they are inherited from the parents. One set is inherited from the mother and one set is inherited from the father.

9. Alleles, genotypes and phenotypes

1 B

2 (a) A phenotype is a visible characteristic that does not change.
  (b) *Example answer:* Brown hair.
  (c) A person's phenotype is determined by their genes. Genes from parents are passed onto their offspring, which explains similarities in phenotype within families.

3 Heterozygous means different so if a person is heterozygous for a gene, it means that they have different alleles of the same gene.

10. Punnett squares and pedigree diagrams

1 B

2 The characteristic from a recessive allele will only be seen if two copies of the allele are present in the genotype.

3 (a)

		Female gametes	
		D	d
Male gametes	d	Dd	dd
	d	Dd	dd

  (b) 50%
  (c) D

11. Predicting genetic outcomes

1 (a)

		Female gametes	
		b	b
Male gametes	B	Bb	Bb
	b	bb	bb

  (b) 50%
  (c) Homozygous recessive.

2 (a) D
  (b) Individuals 2 and 3 both have the genotype Cc, as they do not have cystic fibrosis but must both have inherited a recessive allele from their mother. Pedigree analysis will determine the likelihood that their offspring will either inherit or carry cystic fibrosis.
  If both parents are heterozygous (Cc), there is a 25% chance that their offspring will be affected (cc) and a 50% chance that they will be carriers (Cc).
  If one parent is homozygous dominant (CC) and the other heterozygous (Cc), there is a 50% chance that their offspring will be carriers (Cc) and a 50% chance that they will be neither carriers nor sufferers (CC).
  If one parent is homozygous recessive (cc) and the other heterozygous (Cc), there is a 50% chance that their offspring will be affected (cc) and a 50% chance that they will be carriers (Cc).

12. Genetic mutations
1 If part of the base sequence on a DNA molecule is changed this results in changes in the genetic code.
2 The phenotype of an organism can change.
3 (a) *Example answer:* Cystic fibrosis.
   (b) This means that the genetic mutation will only be shown in the phenotype of a person if there are two copies of the recessive allele in their genotype.

Learning aim B
13. Homeostasis
1 B
2 1 Nervous system.
  2 Endocrine system.
3 Processing centre.
4 Exercising causes an increase in the production of carbon dioxide because this is produced as a waste product in respiration.
It also causes body temperature to increase because muscles produce heat when they are contracting.

14. The nervous system
1 (a) D
  (b) C
2 (a) Brain and spinal cord.
  (b) Sensory neurones and motor neurones.
3 (a) A receptor is found in the sense organs and detects a stimulus or change in the environment.
  (b) An effector is a muscle or gland and responds to a stimulus by producing an action or a secretion.

15. Involuntary and voluntary responses
1 A
2 (a) *Example answer:* Dropping a hot object.
  (b) The receptor cells pick up a stimulus and transmits an impulse to the CNS. In the CNS the sensory neurones connect via synapses to motor neurones. The motor neurones then send impulses to the effectors to initiate a response.
3 A voluntary response requires a thought process for the brain to process a response whereas an involuntary response does not involve a thought process. The thought process takes extra time which is why a voluntary response takes longer to initiate than an involuntary response.

16. Synapses
1 B
2 The electrical impulse reaches the synapse at the end of the neurone. This releases a chemical called a neurotransmitter into the gap. This causes a new electrical impulse in the next neurone.
3 (a) A – Nucleus.
      B – Receptor.
      C – Fatty sheath.
      D – Cell body.
  (b) The signal travels along the sensory neurones down their axons as an electrical impulse. This travels across synapses using neurotransmitters to reach the CNS.

17. Control of blood glucose
1 B
2 B
3 (a) The blood glucose concentration goes down between 05.00 and 07.00, rises at 08.00, goes down between 09.00 and 12.00 and begins to rise again at 13.00.
  (b) The blood glucose levels go down as the individual has not had anything to eat during this period. Then they eat a meal which contains carbohydrates so their blood glucose concentration starts to rise. The blood glucose levels start to fall following a meal as the blood glucose is used up for exercise or is stored in the body.
  (c) When blood glucose levels are too high, the pancreas secretes the hormone insulin which acts on the liver to store the excess glucose as glycogen. This returns the blood glucose levels to normal and the pancreas stops secreting insulin.

18. Differences between the endocrine and nervous systems
1 (a) Liver.
  (b) It is secreted into and carried in the blood stream.
2 A
3 The endocrine system transmits signals via a gland secreting a hormone which is carried in the blood so the speed of communication is slow. The nervous system transmits signals via electrical impulses that are transmitted along neurones and chemical transmission across nerve synapses so the speed of communication is faster than the endocrine system.

19. Thermoregulation
1 B
2 Goose bumps make a person's body hair stand up. This helps to reduce heat loss by trapping a layer of insulating air next to the skin, so slowing heat loss.
3 Receptors in the brain detect changes in blood temperature, whilst receptors in the skin detect changes in skin temperature.
4 It is important for body temperature to stay at 37°C as chemical reactions in the body work best at this temperature.
5 Sweating helps the body to lose heat by releasing sweat onto the skin. When this liquid evaporates it takes heat from the surface and so cools down the skin and the blood next to it. Vasodilation also helps the body to lose heat. This is when blood vessels close to the skin surface widen, or dilate. The blood then loses heat by radiation.

20. Learning aim B: 6-mark questions 1
1 The increase in temperature is detected by heat receptors in the skin which detect a change in skin temperature and receptors in the brain which detect a change in blood temperature.
When the body detects that it is too hot it responds in three main ways to try to reduce the body temperature.
  1 Body hair is lowered which increases heat loss from the skin.
  2 Blood vessels close to the skin surface dilate (vasodilation) so blood is brought closer to the skin surface and excess body heat is lost to the environment.
  3 The body also produces sweat. The evaporation of sweat on the skin causes heat to be lost.
When the person stops exercising, the receptors in the skin and brain detect that the body is cooling down which will then slow the sweating rate down and eventually stop it, and the blood vessels leading to the skin surface will constrict to prevent excess heat loss and maintain the body's core temperature at 37°C.

21. Learning aim B: 6-mark questions 2
1 The endocrine system is used mainly to maintain homeostasis, whereas the nervous system allows the body to respond instantly to a change in the environment. Both systems contain effectors which produce responses to any change. In the nervous system, the effectors are muscles. They produce a movement in response to a nervous impulse. In the endocrine system, the effectors are glands. They secrete a hormone which produces a response in the target organ. For example, the pancreas is a gland which secretes insulin when blood sugar levels are too high. This insulin targets the liver which responds by storing the excess blood sugar. The two systems transmit their information in very different ways. The nervous system has a much faster method of transferring information which can take less than a second. The nervous system sends electrical impulses along nerve cells, and a chemical signal is used across the synapse to trigger the electrical impulse along the next neurone. In the endocrine system, it takes much longer for the response to occur. The gland releases a hormone which travels in the blood stream to the target organ, and the target organ then initiates a response. This all takes some time. As a result, the effects of the endocrine system also last a long time, lasting minutes, hours or days, whereas the duration of the effects of the nervous system is less than a second.

Learning aim C
22. The structure of an atom 1
1 D
2 **(a)** 1 Electrons.
2 Protons.
3 Neutrons.
(b) Protons and neutrons are found in the nucleus of an atom.
(c)

23. The structure of an atom 2
1 **(a)** Negative.
(b) Neutral/no charge.
(c) Electrons are arranged in electron shells surrounding the nucleus.
2

Atom	Electrons	Neutrons	Protons
Sodium	11	12	11
Oxygen	8	8	8

3 An element is made up of lots of the same type of atom.
4 D

24. Atomic number and mass number
1 **(a)** 6
(b) 0 / neutral.
2 **(a)** The mass number (or the number of protons plus neutrons).
(b) The atomic number (or the number of protons).
3 **(a)** 10
(b) 10
(c) 10

25. The periodic table 1
1 C
2 **(a)** Groups.
(b) Periods.
(c) Elements in vertical columns have the same number of electrons in their outer shell.
3 D
4 The elements are arranged in rows in order of increasing atomic number. These are placed in order of increasing number of protons. The elements are also arranged into one of 8 groups which are in columns in the periodic table. In each group the elements have similar chemical properties.
The elements are also arranged so that the left-hand side of the periodic table are all metallic elements and then a zig zag line starting from boron, separates the metals from the non metals, which are on the right-hand side.

26. The periodic table 2
1 A Beryllium B Carbon C Sulfur
D Argon E Calcium F Copper
G Bromine
2 **(i)** Lithium **(ii)** Sodium **(iii)** Oxygen
(iv) Zinc **(v)** Hydrogen

27. Isotopes and relative atomic mass
1 C
2 The relative atomic mass of an element is the average mass of a large number of atoms of the element and is affected by the percentage abundance of each isotope of an element.
3 **(a)** 5
(b) $[(20 \times 10) + (80 \times 11)] / 100$
$= 10.8$

28. Filling electron shells 1
1 C
2 B

3 **(a)**

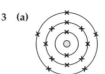

(b) 2.8.5
4 **(a)**

(b) 2.8.2

29. Filling electron shells 2
1 **(a)**

(b) 2.8.8.2
2 **(a)** **(b)** **(c)**

(d) **(e)** **(f)**

3 **(a)** 2.2
(b) 2
(c) 2.8.8.2
(d) 2.8.1
(e) 2.8.4
(f) 2.8.8

30. Electron shells and groups
1 C
2 **(a)** 1 They all have similar properties to each other.
2 They all have complete outer electron shells.
(b)

Group 3	Atomic number	Electronic configuration
$^{7}_{3}$Li	3	2.1
$^{23}_{11}$Na	11	2.8.1
$^{39}_{19}$K	19	2.8.8.1

3 **(a)** It would be in Group 6 of the periodic table because it has 6 electrons in its outer shell.
(b) It would be in Group 5 of the periodic table because it has 5 electrons in its outer shell.

31. Metals and non-metals
1 **(a)** A
(b) C
2 Non-metals appear on the right-hand side of the periodic table. Metals are on the left-hand side of the periodic table. The metals and non-metals are separated by a zig zag line starting from boron.

Learning aim D
32. Compounds and formulae
1 **(a)** Li – Lithium
Na – Sodium
C – Carbon
(b) Hydrogen – H
Potassium – K
Copper – Cu
2 **(a)** 1 sulfur atom.
(b) 4 oxygen atoms.

3

Atom name	Number of atoms
calcium	1
nitrogen	2
oxygen	6

33. Elements, compounds and mixtures

1 B
2 (a) *Example answer:* Chlorine.
  (b) A molecule is when two or more atoms are bonded together.
3 A mixture contains a number of different substances that are combined but not bonded together. This means that mixtures can be quite easily split up into their constituents using physical processes.
  A compound contains two or more different types of atom that are joined together by chemical bonds. They can only be split into their constituent parts by chemical reactions.

34. Word equations

1 (a) (i) Reactants are the substances that take part in a reaction.
      (ii) A product is new substance formed by a chemical reaction.
  (b) carbon + oxygen → carbon dioxide
  (c) hydrogen + oxygen → water
2 B
3 (a) zinc + hydrochloric acid → zinc chloride + water + hydrogen
  (b) sodium hydroxide + hydrochloric acid → sodium chloride + water
  (c) iron + hydrochloric acid → iron chloride + hydrogen
  (d) magnesium + sulfuric acid → magnesium sulfate + hydrogen

35. Balanced chemical equations

1 (a) $Mg + 2HCl \rightarrow MgCl_2 + H_2$
  (b) $CuO + 2HCl \rightarrow CuCl_2 + H_2O$
  (c) $H_2SO_4 + 2NAOH \rightarrow Na_2SO_4 + 2H_2O$
2 (a) $ZnO + 2HNO_3 \rightarrow Zn(NO_3)_2 + H_2O$
  (b) $2HCl + CuCO_3 \rightarrow CuCl_2 + CO_2 + H_2O$
  (c) $H_2SO_4 + 2NaOH \rightarrow 2H_2O + Na_2SO_4$
3 B
4

Atom	Number
Zn	1
N	2
O	6

36. Acids, bases and alkalis

1 C
2 A
3 A – Akali.
  B – Neutral.
  C – Acid.
4 (a) *Example answer:* Copper oxide.
  (b) Most bases will not dissolve in water. An alkali is a type of base that does dissolve in water.

37. Neutralisation reactions

1 B
2 (a) acid + base → salt + water
  (b) nitric acid + sodium hydroxide → sodium nitrate + water
3 If too much acid or base is added there will be no neutralisation reaction, as too much acid will mean that the product remains acidic. If too much base is added then the product will remain alkaline.
4 (a) B
  (b) D
5 (a) A salt and water.
  (b) (i) zinc oxide + hydrochloric acid → zinc chloride + water
      (ii) copper oxide + nitric acid → copper nitrate + water
      (iii) copper oxide + sulfuric acid → copper sulfate + water

38. Equations for neutralisation reactions

1 nitric acid + sodium hydroxide → sodium nitrate + water
2 (a) A salt and water.
  (b) (i) copper oxide + hydrochloric acid → copper chloride+ water
      (ii) copper oxide + nitric acid → copper nitrate + water
      (iii) copper oxide + sulfuric acid → copper sulfate + water
3 The pH of an acid is less than 7, so when an alkali is added to it the pH will increase, because an alkali has a pH of more than 7.

39. Reactions of acids with metals

1 acid + metal → a salt + hydrogen
2 A
3 (a) zinc + hydrochloric acid → zinc chloride + hydrogen
  (b) magnesium + sulfuric acid → magnesium sulfate + hydrogen
  (c) iron + hydrochloric acid → iron chloride + hydrogen
4 (a) Chloride.
  (b) Sulfate.
  (c) Nitrate.

40. Reactions of acids with carbonates

1 1 A salt.
  2 Carbon dioxide.
  3 Water.
2 Bubbles form which show that a gas has been produced in the reaction.
3 (a) sulfuric acid + sodium carbonate → sodium sulfate + water + carbon dioxide
  (b) hydrochloric acid + copper carbonate → copper chloride + water + carbon dioxide
  (c) nitric acid + calcium carbonate → calcium nitrate + water + carbon dioxide

41. Tests for hydrogen and carbon dioxide

1 (a) B
  (b) A
2 The reaction of an acid and a carbonate produces carbon dioxide. This gas produced in the reaction goes into the limewater and is bubbled through it, if the limewater turns cloudy it confirms that the gas is carbon dioxide.
3 An acid and a metal react to produce hydrogen. To test if this gas has been produced, place a lighted wooden splint into the test tube that contains the gas. If hydrogen is present there will be a popping sound because the gas will ignite.

42. Hazard symbols

1 (a) Toxic.
  (b) Corrosive.
  (c) Flammable.
  (d) Moderate hazard.
  (e) Environmental hazard.
2 As lots of chemicals can be harmful, these are given easily recognised symbols that are the same all over the world. This is so that people from different countries who speak different languages will be able to recognise the symbols and know to be careful when handling these substances.
3 (a) Avoid contact with the skin and eyes.
  (b) *Example answer:* Strong acids or strong bases.

43. Applications of neutralisation reactions

1 B
2 Acid rain can change the pH of water and soil so that it becomes more acidic. If the water in ponds and lakes becomes more acidic it can cause harm to the fish and plants that live in the water and can even lead to the fish dying if the water becomes too acidic. If soil becomes acidic it can prevent some plants from growing in the soil which is a problem for farmers who wish to grow certain types of crops in their fields.
  The pH of water and soil can be restored by adding lime to the soil and water. This will neutralise the acid, making water and soil less acidic.

44. Learning aim D: 6-mark questions 1

1 Sand and water and iron sulfate are all made up of different elements. An element is made up of only one type of atom. Each element is unique and has its own chemical and physical properties. Sand and water is a mixture which means it is made where two or more elements or compounds are combined together but are not joined together by chemical bonds. This means the chemical properties of the elements or compounds do not change in a mixture. So sand can be separated from water and their properties remain the same as they were before they were mixed.

Iron sulfate is a compound. A compound is formed by two or more elements that have reacted and joined together. In this case, iron, sulfur and oxygen. The elements are bound together by chemical bonds. This means that the chemical and physical properties of the elements will have altered.

45. Learning aim D: 6-mark questions 2

1 A balanced chemical equation shows the numbers and types of atoms involved in a chemical reaction. In a chemical reaction, the atoms involved are not created nor destroyed so the numbers of atoms of the same type on either side of the equation have to be the same. To balance a chemical equation, you should add up the number of atoms on each side of the equation to make sure they are the same.

If they are not, you insert a number at the front of the formula of the reactants and products where needed. When balancing chemical equations, change only the numbers at the front of the chemical symbols. You should never change the small numbers (subscripts) in a chemical equation as this would change the actual formula of the substance.

This equation is not balanced because there are not the same numbers of atoms of each element on each side of the equation.

$$Mg + HCl \rightarrow MgCl_2 + H_2$$

Mg = 1 atom	Mg = 1 atom
H = 1 atom	H = 2 atoms
Cl = 1 atom	Cl = 2 atoms

There is one atom of hydrogen and one atom of chlorine on the left hand side of the equation but 2 atoms of each on the right hand side of the equation. To make the equation balance it is necessary to increase the number of atoms of hydrogen and chlorine on the left hand side of the equation.

$$Mg + 2HCl \rightarrow MgCl_2 + H_2$$

Mg = 1 atom	Mg = 1 atom
H = 2 atom	H = 2 atoms
Cl = 2 atom	Cl = 2 atoms

The equation is now balanced as there are the same numbers of magnesium, hydrogen and chlorine atoms on both the left and right hand sides of the equation.

46. Balanced equations for reactions with acids

1 (a) $2HNO_3 + CaCO_3 \rightarrow Ca(NO_3)_2 + H_2O + CO_2$
  (b) $H_2SO_4 + CaCO_3 \rightarrow CaSO_4 + H_2O + CO_2$
  (c) $2HCl + CaCO_3 \rightarrow CaCl_2 + H_2O + CO_2$
  (d) $H_2SO_4 + Na_2CO_3 \rightarrow Na_2SO_4 + H_2O + CO_2$
  (e) $2HCl + Na_2CO_3 \rightarrow 2NaCl + H_2O + CO_2$
  (f) $H_2SO_4 + 2NaOH \rightarrow Na_2SO_4 + 2H_2O$
  (g) $CuO + 2HCl \rightarrow CuCl_2 + H_2O$
  (h) $Mg + 2HCl \rightarrow MgCl_2 + H_2$
  (i) $Ca + H_2SO_4 \rightarrow CaSO_4 + H_2$
  (j) $Zn + 2HNO_3 \rightarrow Zn(NO_3)_2 + H_2$
  (k) $ZnO + 2HNO_3 \rightarrow Zn(NO_3)_2 + H_2O$

Learning aim E

47. Forms of energy

1 (a) Thermal energy.
  (b) Light energy.
  (c) Sound energy.

2 A vacuum cleaner uses electrical energy to produce mechanical (or kinetic) energy to suck up the dust from carpets. It also produces sound and thermal energy when it is in use.

3 Solar energy only comes from the Sun. Light energy can also come from an artificial light source, such as a torch.

48. Uses of energy

1 (a) *Example answer:* Domestic heating.
  (b) *Example answer:* Washing machine.
  (c) *Example answer:* Telephone.
2 (a) Kinetic energy.
  (b) Gravitational potential energy.
3 Chemical energy → kinetic energy and thermal energy

49. Energy stores

1 C
2 Batteries store chemical energy which can then be transferred into electrical energy to power the toys.
3 A – Elastic potential energy.
  B – Kinetic energy.

50. Thermal energy transfers

1 (a) B
  (b) B
2 (a) Heat is transferred from the hob to the saucepan by conduction. Metal is a good conductor of heat which means the heat will transfer quickly from one end of the material to the other.
  (b) Wood is a poor conductor of heat so it will not heat up much when the saucepan is heated and can be safely handled.
  (c) When a fluid is heated it expands. The fluid becomes less dense and rises. The warm fluid is replaced by cooler, denser fluid which results in a convection current. This transfers energy throughout the fluid.

51. Measuring energy

1 C
2 (a) 20 J
  (b) efficiency $= \dfrac{15 + 5}{40} \times 100$

  $= 50\%$
  (c) People would buy the new plasma television because it uses less power and lasts longer which offsets the higher price when compared with the LC TV.
  $(800/5000) / (1500/20000) = 0.16/0.075 = 2.13$ times more cost-effective over time.

52. Power

1 C
2 (a) 15 minutes = 900 seconds

  $$Power = \frac{55000}{900}$$

  $= 61\,W$
  (b) Energy = power × time
  Energy = 25 W × 5 seconds
  $= 125\,J$
3 Power is a measure of how quickly energy is transferred. If a person runs 1 km on a treadmill they will transfer mechanical energy more quickly and hence use more power than walking 1 km on the treadmill.

53. Paying for electricity

1 (a) 35 kWh
  (b) $35 \times 8p = £2.80$
  (c) $9 \times 3 = 27\,kWh.$
2 The weekly power consumption of the low power heater is:
  $0.9 \times 40 = 36\,kWh$
  Therefore the weekly cost of the low power heater is:
  $36 \times 0.12 = £4.32$
  The weekly power consumption of the high power heater is:
  $2 \times 30 = 60\,kWh$

Therefore the weekly cost of the high power heater is:
$60 \times 0.12 = £7.20$
Conclusion: the school should buy the low power heater as this will result in lower electricity costs despite running for longer.

54. Efficiency of energy transfers

1 (a) This is when the transfer of energy from one form to another does not produce a lot of wasted energy.
  (b) When energy is transferred some energy will always be wasted. Wasted energy occurs when some of the transferred energy is transferred into a form of energy that is not useful.

2 (a) Electrical energy is transferred into sound energy and thermal energy.
  (b) Electrical energy is transferred to thermal energy and light energy.
  (c) The book has gravitational potential energy which is transferred into kinetic energy as the book falls off the shelf and falls to the ground, when the book hits the ground some of the kinetic energy transforms to sound energy and the rest transforms into thermal energy.

3 (a) $\dfrac{350}{800} \times 100 = 43.75\%$

  (b) $\dfrac{30}{50} \times 100 = 60\%$

  (c) $\dfrac{600}{1000} \times 100 = 60\%$

  (d) $\dfrac{250}{400} \times 100 = 62.50\%$

55. Renewable energy resources

1 Renewable energy resources are sources of energy that will not run out because they are continually replaced.
2 B
3 (a) Wind turbines transform kinetic energy of the wind directly into electrical energy.
  (b) Hydroelectric power stations transform gravitational potential energy of stored water into kinetic energy of falling water and then into electrical energy.
  (c) Tidal power transforms kinetic energy of tidal currents or the rise and fall of the tide directly into electrical energy.
4 The environmental benefit of solar power is that there is less use of fossil fuels to generate electricity. This will reduce the amount of pollution that is produced from burning fossil fuels.
5 Hydroelectric power stations use renewable energy sources and do not produce pollution such as sulfur or carbon dioxide. The running costs for hydroelectric power stations may be cheaper.

56. Non-renewable energy resources

1 This means that once the energy resource has been used up they cannot be replaced.
2 (a) (i) A
     (ii) B
  (b) The production of nuclear energy produces radioactive waste which will remain harmful to humans and animals for millions of years. This waste has to be removed and stored safely to prevent damage to the environment which is costly. If there are any leaks, the radioactive materials can cause a lot of damage to people and the environment.
3 The advantages of using gas is that it has much lower set-up costs compared to solar power. Gas will generate electricity 24 hours a day regardless of weather whereas solar power will not generate electricity during the night or when it is very cloudy. The disadvantages are that the gas fuel costs money whereas solar power is free, and the generation of electricity by gas produces pollution which can harm the environment, unlike solar power.

57. Using energy effectively

1 *Example answer:* Use energy efficient light bulbs, turn off appliances rather than leave them on standby and insulate the loft to prevent heat from escaping.
2 The production of electrical energy using non-renewable energy resources produces pollution which is harmful to the environment. Reducing electrical energy use will reduce the amount of pollution produced which will reduce the harmful effects to the environment.
3 This means that energy can only be transferred from one form to another or moved, more energy cannot be produced and energy cannot be got rid of.
4 B

58. Learning aim E: 6-mark questions 1

1 In a rollercoaster ride, electrical energy is used initially and transferred into mechanical energy. This is how the rollercoaster car is pulled up the incline at the start of the ride.
At the top of the incline, the car has gravitational potential energy. Gravitational potential energy is energy that is stored in an object because of its position. As the car is high up on the tracks, it has a lot of this type of energy. Then as the cart moves down the track the gravitational potential energy is transformed into kinetic energy and the car speeds up.
The wheels of the car and the track get hot as some of the gravitational potential energy is also transformed into thermal energy. There is also some energy transferred into sound energy as some noise is made as the cart runs along the rails. At the end of the ride, the brakes are applied and some of the kinetic energy is transferred into more heat and sound energy. The car then comes to a standstill as the ride ends.

59. Learning aim E: 6-mark questions 2

1 The following calculations are carried out to find the cost of running each computer for the 300 day period:

Laptop A
kWh = 0.045 kW × 8 h = 0.36 kWh
Electricity cost per day = 0.36 kWh × 19p = 6.84p
Electricity cost per 300 days = £0.0684 × 300 = £20.52

Laptop B
kWh = 0.02 kW × 8 h = 0.16 kWh
Electricity cost per day = 0.16 kWh × 19p = 3.04p
Electricity cost per 300 days = £0.0304 × 300 = £9.12

There is only £10 difference in price between the two laptops and laptop A is the cheaper of the two. However, the laptops are different wattages. The wattage of an appliance is the amount of energy transferred by that appliance. A larger wattage means that a greater amount of energy is transferred and more electricity needs to be provided for the appliance to work.
The cost of electricity for laptop A is greater than that for laptop B by £11.40. This means that it is actually £1.40 cheaper for Simon to buy laptop B as its running costs are less than the running costs for laptop A.

Learning aim F
60. Wave characteristics

1 (a)

  (b) (i) A
     (ii) B
2 (a) Wavelength is the distance from the peak of one wave to the peak of the next wave.
  (b) Metres.

61. Wave calculations

1 C

2 (a) wave speed = $10 \times 50 = 500\,\text{m/s}$

   (b) Frequency = wave speed/wavelength

$$= \frac{300}{30}$$

$$= 10\,\text{Hz}$$

   (c) wavelength = wave speed/frequency

$$= \frac{500}{40}$$

$$= 12.5\,\text{m}$$

3 Wave A wave speed = 15×10

$$= 150\,\text{m/s}$$

  Wave B wave speed = 20×15

$$= 300\,\text{m/s}$$

  Wave B has the fastest wave speed.

62. The electromagnetic spectrum

1 A

2 Frequency = wave speed/wave length

$$= \frac{80}{10}$$

$$= 8\,\text{Hz}$$

3 A – UV rays.
  B – X-rays.
  C – Microwaves.
  D – Radio waves.

4

Radio waves	Microwaves	Infrared	Visible light	Ultraviolet	X-rays	Gamma rays

63. Radio waves

1 D

2 (a) They are placed at the end with the lowest frequency.

   (b) Radio waves are mainly used for different methods of communication by transmitting information 'wirelessly' through the air. They are also used for radar, to detect the presence of objects in the air.

   (c) The higher the frequency of the wave the more energy the wave can transfer which can cause harm to humans. Radio waves have the lowest frequency in the electromagnetic spectrum so do not cause any harm to humans.

   (d) wave speed = frequency × wave length

$$= 10 \times 15$$

$$= 150\,\text{m/s}$$

64. Microwaves

1 B

2 (a) B

   (b) Wave speed = wave length × frequency

$$= 0.125 \times 2\,400\,000\,000$$

$$= 300\,000\,000\,\text{m/s}$$

   (c) *Example answer:* 1 Mobile phones.
                      2 Satellite television.

65. Infrared radiation

1 C

2 (a) *Example answer:* 1 Toaster.
                      2 High speed internet access.
                      3 Cable TV.

   (b) Short infrared waves do not cause any heating, but long infrared waves do.
     The TV remote control uses short infrared waves so it does not have a heating effect and will not harm a person. Grills use long infrared waves which do have a heating affect and will burn a person if they get too close.

66. Visible light

1 C

2

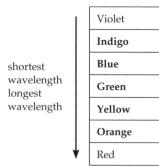

shortest wavelength	Violet
	Indigo
	Blue
	Green
longest wavelength	Yellow
	Orange
	Red

3 Visible light is reflected from objects to allow our eyes to see them and photography works in the same way. The visible light enters the camera through an aperture and lands on a detector. This detector converts the light energy into electrical energy so the image can be stored digitally.

67. Ultraviolet light

1 B

2 *Example answer:* 1 Detecting forged bank notes.
                      2 Disinfecting water.

3 Excess exposure to UV light can cause sunburn which damages the skin and can lead to skin cancer. Excess exposure to UV light can also damage the eyes and cause cataracts.

4 Water may contain bacteria which are living cells and may be harmful to humans. By using high levels of ultraviolet light on the water, this will kill the bacteria as they are living cells and therefore disinfect the water.

68. X-rays

1 *Example answer:* 1 Medical use, for example to detect damaged bones.
                      2 Security use, for example baggage scanners to check for prohibited items.

2 (a) *Example answer:* 1 Cancer.
                          2 Infertility.

   (b) X-rays have a high frequency that is harmful to humans and can cause cancer. The lead apron prevents the X-rays from coming into contact with the radiographer.

69. Gamma rays

1 (a) C

   (b) C

2 (a) Gamma rays have a very high frequency and therefore carry high energy which means they can damage or kill living cells. Cancer is caused by damaged cells and therefore could be caused by gamma rays, but if the gamma rays are targeted properly they can kill the cancer cells.

   (b) A doctor would have to wear something that would shield their body from the gamma rays and stop the rays from penetrating through the equipment. A thick lead shielding would provide this protection from gamma rays.

Your own notes

Published by Pearson Education Limited, Edinburgh Gate, Harlow, Essex, CM20 2JE.

www.pearsonschoolsandfecolleges.co.uk

Copies of official specifications for all BTEC qualifications may be found on the Edexcel website: www. edexcel.com

Text and original illustrations © Pearson Education Limited 2013
Edited, produced, typeset and illustrated by Wearset Limited, Boldon, Tyne and Wear
Cover illustration by Miriam Sturdee

First published 2013

17 16 15 14 13
10 9 8 7 6 5 4 3

British Library Cataloguing in Publication Data
A catalogue record for this book is available from the British Library

ISBN 978 1 446 90278 3

Printed in Slovakia by Neografia

Acknowledgements
The author and publisher would like to thank the following individuals and organisations for permission to reproduce photographs:
(Key: b-bottom; c-centre; l-left; r-right; t-top)
Alamy Images: i love images / men's lifestyle 67, Neil McAllister 62tl; **Digital Vision:** 56; **Pearson Education Ltd:** Jon Barlow 47; **Science Photo Library Ltd:** Gary Retherford 68, Health Protection Agency 69; **Shutterstock.com:** bloomua 62bl, Evgeny Karandaev 65r, Francesco81 65l, Helder Almeida 20, Maridav 13, Mihai M 62br, wavebreakmedia 40, Yuri Arcurs 62tr; **Veer/Corbis:** diego cervo 48, flashon 52l, 52r, irabel8 33, Monkey Business Images 36, Qingwa 10; **www.imagesource.com:** 66

All other images © Pearson Education

In some instances we have been unable to trace the owners of copyright material, and we would appreciate any information that would enable us to do so.

In the writing of this book, no BTEC examiners authored sections relevant to examination papers for which they have responsibility.